Contents

CW01507955

RESET YOUR HOME

RESET YOUR HOME

Unpack your emotions and your clutter, step by step

LESLEY SPELLMAN
WITH
INGRID JANSEN

GREEN TREE
LONDON • OXFORD • NEW YORK • NEW DELHI • SYDNEY

GREEN TREE
Bloomsbury Publishing Plc
50 Bedford Square, London, WC1B 3DP, UK
Bloomsbury Publishing Ireland Limited
29 Earlsfort Terrace, Dublin 2, D02 AY28, Ireland

BLOOMSBURY, GREEN TREE and the Green Tree logo are trademarks of
Bloomsbury Publishing Plc

First published in Great Britain 2025
Copyright © Lesley Spellman and Ingrid Jansen, 2025
Illustrations © Luke Spellman, 2025

A catalogue record for this book is available from the British Library

Library of Congress Cataloguing-in-Publication data has been applied for

ISBN: TPB: 978-1-3994-1639-9; ePUB: 978-1-3994-1642-9; ePDF: 978-1-3994-1641-2

2 4 6 8 10 9 7 5 3 1

Typeset in Minion by Deanta Global Publishing Services, Chennai, India
Printed and bound in Great Britain by CPI Group (UK) Ltd, Croydon, CRO 4YY

To find out more about our authors and books visit www.bloomsbury.com
and sign up for our newsletters

For product safety related questions contact productsafety@bloomsbury.com

To anyone who has ever felt overwhelmed, judged, embarrassed, guilty or stuck because of the things in their home, this book is for you.

1

Emotions first, stuff second

Stuff is a funny old thing, isn't it? As simple as it ought to be, it's not. It's complex.

We need stuff to support our lives. It's essential, helpful and functional. We use stuff every single day and we love having it around us. It's pleasurable, emotive and grounding. There's no question that stuff can absolutely enhance a happy home.

But it can also detract ... hugely. That stuff that was once beneficial can at a later date serve no practical purpose in our homes. And that stuff that once made us smile might since have been replaced by other much more special stuff.

Decluttering and organising your home can change your life. It sounds dramatic but as professional organisers, with over 28 years of experience between us, we know it's true. Once you nail it, you'll never look back. Your home should provide the building blocks for a calm, happy and fulfilled life, and the stuff you choose to have around you needs to make those foundations stronger.

The decluttering process is all about finding the good stuff among the not-so-good. Sounds like a straightforward undertaking, right? If only it were that simple. Let us ask you some important questions to get you thinking:

- Have you embarked on a decluttering journey more times than you care to mention?
- Have you had some success, but the clutter keeps on coming back?

9

- Perhaps you've put in your best effort, but you've struggled to keep up momentum?
- Or maybe you've failed to get off the decluttering starting blocks because it all seems so overwhelming?

We suspect everyone reading this can relate to at least one of the above. This shows that decluttering is, in fact, not straightforward at all.

The reason you've struggled in the past, more than likely, is ironically because you've focused too much on the 'stuff'. You see most people, when decluttering, focus primarily on the 'things': the items, the bags of items, the piles of items. But the secret here is that decluttering is never really about the stuff... Let us explain.

We've developed our Reset Your Home system to flip this focus on 'stuff' on its head. Instead, first and foremost, our system allows you to focus on the *emotions* that sit behind the stuff. This is because we understand that once you have worked out how your emotional connection to clutter is holding you back, then letting go of the actual stuff becomes a breeze. Emotions first, stuff second. Always.

But before we explain this further, we think it's time to introduce ourselves.

Who are we?

We are Ingrid and Lesley, and we have both helped thousands of people from all walks of life in our roles as professional organisers. We met in 2011 at the very first conference for the UK Association of Professional Declutterers and Organisers (APDO), over a coffee and a chocolate chip cookie. We had an immediate chemistry and a shared vision for encouraging the 'right' kind of people to join the organising and decluttering industry. By this we mean that it's very important to us that professional organisers not only know how to help clear clutter from homes but also how to empathise and unravel their clients' deeply rooted connection to their things.

For four years we both had volunteer roles on the Board of APDO: Ingrid was the president and Lesley was head of mentoring. Through this, we learned about the power of community and teamwork and, most importantly, we became advocates for the benefits of living a clutter-free life.

When our volunteering days came to a natural end with APDO, we weren't ready to stop working together, so we cooked up a plan to do something collaboratively online. We'd both been working one to one with clients in their homes for years, but there were still so many people we wanted to help but couldn't reach. We were both very good at talking, that's for sure, so we decided that rather than chatting on the phone for hours on end to each other, maybe chatting on a podcast to other people – about our shared love of decluttering – might be a better use of our time. That's how our weekly podcast (*The Declutter Hub Podcast*) was born. It didn't take long for us to realise that our listeners resonated with what we had to say about the *emotional connection* many of us have to the things in our homes. So we kept on talking!

Some of our listeners needed more structure, guidance and personal input from us when it came to their decluttering journeys, which is why our Declutter Hub membership and wider online community started to evolve. It was at this point that our Reset Your Home system – which is what we'll be walking you through in this book – was developed.

The system has been fundamentally shaped by those who have asked for our help. Every story, every struggle, every tear, every breakthrough we've encountered from those we are privileged to have helped taught us that unravelling our deep relationship with the 'things' in our homes is the key to long-term decluttering success. We'll say it again: emotions first, stuff second.

We had no idea that our little idea for a podcast was going to blossom into something bigger and better than we could ever have imagined. For the last decade, we have been able to make an impact in homes from Brisbane to Bristol, from Wellington to Winnipeg, from Cork to Chicago, each and every day through our weekly podcast, membership and online community (details are on p. 250 if you'd like to know more). This is something we never ever take for granted.

We smile from ear to ear each time we see a success story. After all, what's not to like about someone changing from being overwhelmed to overjoyed?

The one request we've had repeatedly from our members and listeners is that we write a book. What better way could there be to bring all the tips, tools and teaching together into one easy-to-access place, so that more and more people can start to live a life with less clutter? So, this book is our response to that request. We do hope you enjoy it.

Lesley: Why I became a professional organiser

Back in 2009, I had just finished an 18-month-long renovation of a derelict Victorian home for my family to move into. The neighbours were delighted to see the eyesore that had existed for decades being restored to its former glory. While it was so lovely to have people say positive things about the work that we had done, the discussions about the person who had lived in our home previously were judgemental, harsh and negative. While it's unlikely that there had been a clinical diagnosis, the man who had lived there almost certainly had what I now know to be hoarding disorder. And boy oh boy did the negative judgements about the way he lived keep on coming. Each and every conversation at our front gate demonstrated no acknowledgement of the human behind the clutter and the struggles he was obviously facing.

Those interactions had such an impact on me that the seed was sown to set up a business to help people not only physically but emotionally eradicate the clutter from their homes. Within a few months, my business, the Clutter Fairy, was launched and ready to work its magic on the cluttered homes of the North West of England. Getting down to the nitty-gritty of the emotional hold clutter has on us has always been where I do my best work.

Ingrid: Why I became a professional organiser

I've spent all my adult life in the business of keeping house. I credit my mum with my early love of all things organising and homemaking, which I enjoyed so much that I developed it into a career in hotel housekeeping. Five-star hotels in my native country, the Netherlands, were where I honed my organising and cleaning skills. (Suffice to say, I'm a dab hand at folding a fitted sheet and creating a towel stack!)

After changing more sheets than I'd care to mention, a move overseas to Dublin with my husband was calling us in our thirties. Having enjoyed everything the Emerald Isle had to offer for a few years, we sailed across the Irish Sea to make a new home in London, and we're still there today. Once I realised that the demands of hotel housekeeping and raising a young family were a little incompatible, I started looking for alternatives. My friends told me I should do something that revolved around organising, and that's when my one-to-one decluttering business, Organise Your House, was born.

I live, eat and breathe decluttering and I'm known for seeing it as it is and saying it as it is! Straight talking seems to work perfectly for my clients. Working on their projects and seeing the veil being lifted after a few short hours together makes me insanely happy.

How This Book Works

So, how is this book going to be your gateway to success? How are we going to help you transform chaos to calm? Well, we are going to introduce you to our Reset Your Home system and encourage you to reframe your thinking and approach when it comes to decluttering. We'll give you an overview of how this works now.

Go Room by Room

One of the most difficult things to work out when decluttering your home is where to start and in which order to tackle the rooms. As the Reset Your Home methodology is based on an emotions-first, stuff-second approach, we have chosen to guide you through your home by starting with the rooms where the emotions are less deep-seated.

You'll hear us referring to building up your **decluttering muscle** regularly throughout this book. Just like doing strength exercises with the muscles in your body, you need to gradually strengthen your metaphorical decluttering muscle too. You need to start small, and practise frequently. Once you have flexed your muscles in the less emotive rooms of your home, you can take on bigger and more challenging rooms more successfully later on in your journey.

JARGON BUSTER

Decluttering muscle – a metaphorical muscle based on your ability to make decluttering decisions, which, over time, starts to build and grow.

For this reason, we begin in the kitchen – a room where many of the decisions we need to make are more practical than emotional and where we are able to build up our decluttering skills without becoming overwhelmed. We then move through the house, room by room, strengthening our decluttering muscle as we go, before ending with sentimental items, which is where our emotional connection to clutter is at its most prevalent. This is where we are challenged with a random assortment of items from different periods of our lives and may struggle to let go. But don't worry, because by this point you'll have honed your craft!

Each room will present different emotions and different practical considerations, and these will be mapped out comprehensively as we progress. We highly recommend, therefore, that you follow the room order we suggest, though it is not prescriptive. If you'd like to deviate from our suggested plan that's not a problem at all, but if you'd like to benefit from all our method has to offer then the room-by-room approach is preferable.

THINK THEN DO

Each chapter covers a different room, and within each room our work will be split into two parts: *The thinking* and *The doing*. We will cover the following in these:

1. **The thinking**: We will work through the key emotions that invariably keep you stuck. We're going to help you prepare emotionally and practically for the task ahead and encourage you to think about your goals for each room.
2. **The doing**: We will guide you step by step through the decluttering process with the help of key questions to consider as you go. We will also discuss categorising, organising and storage options, as well as adding the finishing touches to your newly decluttered space.

We would encourage you to read both the thinking and the doing sections of each chapter before getting started on each room, so you have a full understanding of how things will fit together. Then you can refer back to each section as and when needed, as you work through each room. You might find it useful to have a notepad to hand.

TAKE A MOMENT

At certain points in each chapter, we will encourage you to take stock through our 'Take a moment' features. These are designed to help you pause and reflect on your learnings, your struggles and your progress. Standing back from your work every now and again is important to facilitate those tentative steps towards a permanent change in your clutter mindset, so we encourage you not to skip these!

BREAK OLD HABITS

If you always do what you've always done, you'll always get what you've always got. Let's break that down and explain how this applies to the decluttering world and our Reset Your Home system.

What have you always done in the context of a decluttering journey? Maybe you have always focused on the stuff first and foremost. Maybe you have constantly been on the lookout for quick fixes, **flitting** from one decluttering hack to another. Maybe you have been confused by all the conflicting advice out there. Whatever methodology you have come across in the past, it hasn't resonated enough to be cemented sufficiently and provide you with the clutter-free home you deserve. What you have always got in the past is a home where the clutter keeps coming back. It might have happened five years after you last decluttered, it might have taken five months, it might have taken five days but, whatever the timescale, you have not succeeded in altering your clutter mindset sufficiently. That's why you're here, ready and eager for change.

JARGON BUSTER

Flitting – the act of starting decluttering in one room only to become distracted and move your attention to another room, and then another, meaning the original project is abandoned or neglected.

The aim of our Reset Your Home system is that decluttering, organising and tidying your home ultimately becomes something that just happens regularly for you, without it being a huge, overwhelming undertaking. To make this shift it's a case of breaking old habits, so within our system we invite you to be open to the new ideas and approaches we share with you.

You're in the driving seat here. As William Shakespeare said back in 1599, 'It is not in the stars to hold our destiny but in ourselves,' and although we're pretty sure his wisdom wasn't related to decluttering way back when, it still makes complete sense. You, and only you, can determine how this decluttering journey you are about to embark on will unfold. By taking responsibility for your actions and choices, you can create the future home you desire rather than leaving it to chance.

One thing's for sure: there will be roadblocks and bumps along the way on your decluttering journey, and there may be pesky back-seat drivers too! We'd love to be your valued companion as you go, in the passenger seat right there next to you. Allow us to guide you to your destination, to suggest alternative routes, to consider sensible diversions and to let you know when it's time to take a break.

DON'T DECLUTTER THIS BOOK!

We encourage you not to approach this book as a one-time read. Are you going to master the perfect decluttering journey in one rotation of your home? It's unlikely, so don't put that additional pressure on yourself. Expect and embrace a second pass through your home. Actually, expect multiple passes through your home.

The reality is we will have to re-evaluate the things we keep in our homes on a continual basis forever. As stuff comes in, stuff needs to go out. As we move from one phase of our lives to another, our relationship with things changes. But, once you have built up your decluttering muscle and you return to the same areas again, you will be stronger and more steadfast in knowing why something is no longer serving you in your current life and if it can be decluttered.

By employing this phased approach to your clutter, you will feel in control and confident that the decisions you are making are the right ones. And this book will be there on your shelf ready and waiting as your handy reference point whenever you need it.

So, are you ready to embark on a decluttering journey with a tried-and-tested system and a fresh perspective? We encourage you to be open-minded, patient with yourself, but most of all excited, as it's time to get started. You've got this!

A note before we begin

We'd like to take a moment to acknowledge that every home is different, every person is different, and everyone has their own unique relationship with clutter. You may be a seasoned pro at decluttering or this may be your first foray into this world. Wherever you are, this book has something for you. This is because our Reset Your Home system can be applied whether you live in a studio flat or a mansion, whether you live alone or with five other people. That being said, even though this book is extensive and thorough, it's not possible to mention all eventualities specifically, though the principles we teach are applicable to all.

Also please note that there are a couple of household categories you intentionally won't find covered purely for reasons of space within this book. For example, paperwork and digital decluttering are not included here, since they would need entire books of their own! For a little more on paperwork, please see the appendix on p. 247.

Also, as we begin looking at life and the things we have gathered during it, we will undoubtedly encounter emotions and things that are challenging psychologically. While we are well versed in understanding emotional triggers, we are not trained therapists, so this book is not a replacement for seeking medical advice.

2

Understanding your clutter personality

'Everything starts with self-awareness.'

There are many people right across the world who do not experience an issue with clutter. They have established routines, which means clutter is kept to a minimum and they can keep their homes tidy. This is our ultimate goal for you too, but before we can achieve it, we have to undergo a journey to get there.

Decluttering can feel like a very solitary thing to do, so you can be forgiven for thinking you're the worst case there's ever been or that you're destined to live in a chaotic, cluttered house forever. But we have good news: you're not. We want you to understand that you are seen and heard. People with clutter are all unique but also uncannily similar in some ways.

Over the years, we've identified five distinct types of clutter personality, which we'll run through now. The good news is that all of the traits within these clutter personalities can be overcome using the tools provided in this book. See if you relate to any of them. You may resonate with one type, you may resonate with a couple or you may resonate with them all. (Combination and hybrid clutter personalities are common!)

It's worth mentioning that we wholeheartedly encourage you to only focus on current and future progress on your decluttering journey (without the baggage of the past dragging you down or keeping you paralysed), but before we draw this line in the sand we do encourage a small bit of preparatory work first, because understanding and reflecting on what has brought you to this point with your clutter is a foundational step to moving you forwards.

So, which clutter personality are you? Let's dive into the detail!

Clutter personality 1: The Happy Heaper

The Traits

People who are Happy Heapers think about things deeply. They don't just jump straight in and do something without thinking through the consequences. They often have disparate thoughts going through their mind, multiple projects on the go and numerous people to think about, which – all in all – leads to a disorganised and chaotic home life.

The Happy Heaper may be, or suspect they are, neurodivergent; attention deficit hyperactivity disorder (ADHD) and autism spectrum disorder (ASD) in particular are prevalent in the world of clutter. Often, a diagnosis can help explain why things have become the way they are in your home.

Now, in terms of what the cluttered home of a Happy Heaper looks like, it'll come as no surprise that there will be *heaps* of stuff everywhere. Some of those heaps are quite orderly and comprise things that naturally belong together. But there will be other heaps – that heap of junk mail on the end of the kitchen work surface, that heap of randomness on the coffee table, that heap of bags and boxes in the understairs cupboard – that are there as a result of a frantic and frenzied 'tidy-up'.

The Struggles

Happy Heapers are often very focused on sustainability and the environment: they hate throwing stuff away, want things to go to a good home, spend time trying to find the perfect charity to donate to, and aim to recycle everything meticulously, sometimes to the detriment of their decluttering progress.

We regularly see a propensity towards perfectionism and procrastination with a Happy Heaper. They can get so wrapped up in the detail that they struggle to see the big picture. The Happy Heaper will regularly be found using the latest online hack for folding socks and T-shirts, while ignoring the exploding mound of laundry on the bedroom floor.

The Goals

The Happy Heaper is likely committed to changing their ways and making decluttering progress, so let's consider what goals they might have. Maybe they'd love to spontaneously invite family or friends into their home without needing to do hours of tedious preparation. Or perhaps they want to be able to find things more easily. They know it's in the house, they have a vague idea of where it is, but in which heap?

The Happy Heaper needs to enjoy the decluttering process. And by 'enjoy' we mean feel connected to the learning, feel in control of decisions that they're making, and feel proud of the organisational systems that they're establishing in their home. It's vital for the Happy Heaper to feel a sense of gradual accomplishment; to make slow and steady rather than fast and furious progress. They are then able to contemplate stumbling blocks along the way and come to terms with change in their own time.

You may be nodding in acknowledgement of having these traits or shaking your head in relief that you don't. But never fear, if you don't see yourself in the Happy Heaper, we have four more clutter personalities to throw into the mix.

Clutter personality 2:
The Harassed Housekeeper

The Traits

If you feel like these two words sum you up to a T, you are not alone. There are Harassed Housekeepers everywhere and they feel like they are firmly stuck on the hamster wheel of life. They rush from one task to the next throughout the day and barely have time to take a breath. Toothbrushing to supervise, laundry to keep on top of, meals to throw together, appointments to schedule and be on time for, WhatsApp messages to answer, parents to visit – oh and we've not even mentioned the dynamism they need to bring to their actual job. The Harassed Housekeeper tries their absolute best to keep all the plates firmly spinning but feels any one of them could come crashing down at any moment.

In terms of what the Harassed Housekeeper's home looks like, it's going to be largely governed by who lives with them. But the Harassed Housekeeper is a category not just reserved for people with kids. There are plenty of people from all walks of life who have an abundance of responsibilities that mean that their homes sink lower in the pecking order of priorities. The overwhelm is likely to have developed out of an accumulation of stuff coupled with a struggle to keep on top of daily and weekly chores. So, visibly, their home is likely to appear chaotic but not overly full. There may be areas of the home that are clutter-free and function perfectly well but then there are rooms where things get thrown as a 'temporary' solution and the door is kept firmly closed.

The Harassed Housekeeper shares traits with the Happy Heaper but the key difference is that the Harassed Housekeeper is struggling mostly due to time and capacity, rather than the emotional and psychological barriers a Happy Heaper encounters.

The Struggles

The Harassed Housekeeper is likely to be cash rich and time poor so may choose to buy things to fix an immediate problem. They have good intentions to create a home-cooked meal but time has just run out on them, so takeaway or a ready meal beckons. They have no idea where the light bulbs are for the lamp that has just blown so they just buy a pack of four new ones for ease. There is such an overwhelming feeling of exhaustion when they have got through the day that the last thing they want to do is chores.

The Harassed Housekeeper may struggle to know how to manage a home. They may have grown up with a parent who was also a

Harassed Housekeeper or, conversely, they may have had everything done for them, so they were never taught the fundamentals of cleaning and tidying. They are likely to feel unsupported by other people in their home and always bear the burden of responsibility, berating themselves for their perceived failure to cope.

The Goals

It's likely that the Harassed Housekeeper will have a clear vision of their goal: less stress, more organisation, more time and a home that facilitates relaxation. They just need the process, the support and the headspace to be able to work towards it.

Is any of this sounding familiar? We have more clutter personalities to introduce before we move onwards and upwards.

Clutter Personality 3: The Kind Keeper

The Traits

Now, the Kind Keeper loves to buy new things but loves to keep the old things too.

We meet many Kind Keepers who are in their mid-fifties and older. These people tend to be sociable, love having people over and like to go shopping as part of their leisure time, probably with family or friends. It's likely that now, or at some point in their life, the Kind Keeper has been financially secure enough to buy nice things without too much thought, and this habit continues today. However, the Kind Keeper is hesitant when it comes to throwing things out. Perhaps as a child their family had very little so they have retained the idea that *everything* could be useful. People who are Kind Keepers are typically sentimental as well. They love to have things in their home that remind them of happy times. But often the amount of 'special' things they have means they are no longer able to find the quality in among the quantity.

But the Kind Keepers don't just belong to older generations. Younger people have grown up with consumerism all around them, which tends to be why younger Kind Keepers regularly like to shop. However, as their family grows and they begin building their life in a home that used to be just for them (but now has to accommodate a family of four), there just isn't room any longer to keep everything.

The Struggles

As we've said, the Kind Keeper loves to buy new things but loves to keep the old things too. And consequently we have a clutter clash.

Any build-up of excess stuff can most certainly lead to issues with other family members, who find the clutter frustrating. This means the Kind Keeper can feel constantly berated for their attachment to things, as tackling clutter becomes a constant topic of conversation. This tension can be draining and damaging to the harmony in the Kind Keeper's home.

The Kind Keeper's sentimentality has a habit of stopping them in their decluttering tracks because everything has a memory attached to it. This means they are constantly adding to their volumes of sentimental items, and any attempts they have made in the past to declutter have been thwarted by constant reminiscing and trips down memory lane. Consequently, it seems as if they're not achieving anything, so they regularly lose faith when decluttering and abandon it as a lost cause.

The Goals

The Kind Keeper needs a goal to drive them through this process. The goals are often related to transitions in their life.

If they are an older Kind Keeper then maybe they want to downsize but aren't sure how to make that happen. Or perhaps they wonder whether their stuff will all just get thrown into a skip once they're gone, and that scares them, so they feel a sense of urgency to do something about it now. Or if they are a younger Kind Keeper then maybe they are keen to grow their family and need to work out how to make room for an extra person amid all the stuff they have amassed.

Because the Kind Keeper is a sociable being, creating a welcoming space that people can visit without judgement and having a harmonious relationship with the people they live with are important factors for them. If the things in their home feel out of control and begin to affect the sociable parts of their life, then what better goal is there than to declutter, so they can reset relationships with those they love?

The desire to create a happy, welcoming home that can ebb and flow through life and its transitions is on many people's wish lists when it comes to decluttering, so there's a good chance you can see some of the Kind Keeper in yourself. However, if you're still trying to work out whether there's a clutter personality that suits you better, read on...

Clutter Personality 4: The Warm Weeper

The Traits

A Warm Weeper really struggles with their emotional connection to stuff, and quite often that struggle emanates from a place of pain or disruption to their life in the past. Maybe it was unkind words that threw them off track and sent them spiralling, or at the other end of the spectrum they may have suffered a serious loss or trauma. Quite often, it's not just one sad or difficult thing that's happened in their life, it's multiple, and it's been a constant battle. Naturally, that trauma has led to an overwhelming and debilitating feeling of melancholy and resulted in tears many times in their life.

The Warm Weeper is likely to use stuff as a form of comfort. Stuff has offered respite from the complications of relationships and memories in the past. Stuff hasn't let them down ... until today. The stuff they have acquired is now so voluminous that it is dragging them down rather than propping them up. They have come to the realisation that where once they wanted stuff, now all they want is space.

The Struggles

Because they have undergone trauma or difficulties in their life, the Warm Weeper does often have people around them who have reached out in the past to help them with their clutter. But sometimes the people who have tried to help haven't respected or understood the depth of the emotional attachment that a Warm Weeper feels to their things. The person who offered help has focused on decluttering ruthlessly and that has sadly done more harm than good.

If the Warm Weeper continues to focus on all the baggage from the past, how can they make space for the future version of themselves? They must do things differently to pay homage to sentimentality while keeping it clearly in perspective.

The Goals

So how does the Warm Weeper make positive progress when things seem so tough? It's vital for them to have a clear picture of where they want to go, how they want their life to change and how their home is going to support that.

One of the big drivers for a Warm Weeper to declutter is to move beyond a constant feeling of being judged. The desire to get it done is strong, so it's all about taking action and becoming accountable so they can work through their clutter in a calm, controlled manner. Focusing on their own goals, dreams and timescales rather than feeling railroaded by someone else's is the key here.

So, do you relate to the Warm Weeper or are you a hybrid or combination clutter personality? We've got another option to chat through, then we'll dig deeper into how to make the necessary steps towards change.

Clutter personality 5: The Nostalgic Knee-deeper

The Traits

Let's first talk about the word 'knee-deeper'. Is it even a word? Maybe not, but it encompasses perfectly the literal and metaphorical picture of what we are aiming to describe. Essentially, the Nostalgic Knee-deeper has the sense that their clutter is all-consuming and it makes them feel they are 'knee-deep' in the clutter in their life.

Consequently, commonplace daily tasks may be compromised. The Nostalgic Knee-deeper may have, or suspect they have, hoarding behaviours or hoarding disorder.

The Nostalgic Knee-deeper feels embarrassed by their clutter. They have probably been subjected to repeated judgement throughout their life, which has led to a conscious choice to safeguard their privacy. They may have shied away from inviting guests into their home and feel panicked when they hear a knock at the front door.

Because clutter – and their attachment to it – has become intrinsically linked to their sense of self, they have become self-deprecating and often use humour when talking about their home.

Equally, the Knee-deeper may not literally have 'knee-deep' clutter but they might be troubled by a much smaller volume of clutter that has built up to such a level that they feel out of control. Whether being 'knee-deep' in clutter is literal or metaphorical, they are likely to feel defined by the clutter in their home.

The Struggles

The Nostalgic Knee-deeper has become resistant to change. They have read the decluttering books, watched the TV programmes and binged the YouTube videos but each time they struggle to make visible headway or keep momentum, so have become disillusioned. While they have a constant and urgent desire to improve their quality of life, they wonder whether the ship has sailed and whether the clutter will continue to be a part of their story for the rest of their life.

This portrayal of a Nostalgic Knee-deeper may seem quite bleak, as if there is no tangible solution, but there absolutely is. The volume of clutter at home may be higher, the emotional attachment may be more persistent, but progress can still be made. It will take longer, it will be harder, but it's no less possible for the Knee-deeper to make solid and positive progress than any of the other types of clutter personality we've described.

The Goals

The Nostalgic Knee-deeper is going to need a goal to get themselves kick-started but this needs to be phased, otherwise the task will seem insurmountable. They need to tackle the job step by step, thought by thought, item by item.

Their foundational goal needs to be about self-belief, about kindness, about letting go of past 'failures'. When the Nostalgic Knee-deeper gives themself permission to work through their clutter their way, in their time and with their own assessment of what progress looks like, the first steps towards a home that supports rather than sabotages their well-being is there for the taking.

TAKE A MOMENT

Do any of the clutter personalities resonate with you? It's very likely that you have elements of several types, or you may feel that one sums you up perfectly.

Take a moment to consider your clutter personality and then use this insight to consider why you want to change now, and think about what barriers you'll need to overcome. Understanding your why is key, as this will be the purpose that drives you forwards along the way.

3

Decluttering 101

'The dos and don'ts of decluttering'

Before we get down to business and tackle our first room, we want to share our dos and don'ts of decluttering. These are the basics that we will be referring to time and again throughout the decluttering journey. We think it'll be helpful for you to have them together in one place here.

Do keep it real

If there is one overarching message that will run throughout this book it's the need to keep things real. Realism is a big part of decluttering and it all stems from understanding yourself and your own limitations. First, we'll share two examples of how realism must show up in decluttering, and then we'll go into much more detail as we begin to explore decluttering room by room in the later chapters.

TRY NOT TO COMPARE YOUR LIVING SPACE

We need to understand that homes come in all different shapes and sizes and, unless a house move is imminent, your home is your home. Therefore, we all need to make the best of our current situation and take realistic decisions based on where we currently live (not where we were before or where we want to be in the future).

The decisions you make about the volumes of items you can keep when you live in a four-bedroom home, for example, will be very different to those available to you when you are living in a studio flat. The space we have is finite and will dictate the choices we need to make. Embrace what you have rather than lamenting what you don't. A realistic assessment and acceptance of the size and make-up of the home you are working with will stand you in good stead for success.

BE MINDFUL OF YOUR HEALTH

Mental health

If you live with poor mental health, it is likely to threaten to sabotage your decluttering efforts. You may be firing on all cylinders for a few weeks and then a sudden bout of depression might knock you for six. Similarly, all the preparation and planning in the world can't stave off sudden and intense anxiety, and menopausal brain fog is a very real and palpable thing for some of us.

Hoarding disorder or hoarding behaviours are especially difficult to navigate and are likely to require psychological intervention alongside any practical strategies in order to facilitate progress.

Neurodiversity

Neurodiversity is also a very common saboteur of our plans for change in our homes. ADHD, ASD and obsessive compulsive disorder (OCD) are common examples of neurodivergence that affect the way we manage the maintenance of our homes.

It's vital to acknowledge our days may become derailed at any point if we have complex mental health needs or are neurodivergent, so the key is to stop when we are struggling and vow to continue when we are feeling brighter and more focused. Realism about what affects us and in what way goes a long way to helping us navigate our decluttering journeys.

Physical health

Similarly, some of us have physical health issues that affect our stamina and impact the logistics of what we can do and where. Fibromyalgia, chronic fatigue syndrome, multiple sclerosis and many more health conditions mean that we must plan differently, ask for help and take our time on projects like this.

We've not even scratched the surface of the many difficulties you may have that can make a decluttering journey more challenging. But remember, if this is you, then your journey may be longer or harder, but if you are realistic about what you can and can't do, and work around this rather than fighting against it, then you will get there.

Do build up your decluttering muscle

DON'T RUN BEFORE YOU CAN WALK

When we think about the decluttering journey that awaits, our minds immediately take us to the trickier areas of our homes: the spare room packed to the brim that we've not used in months; the overflowing bookcases; the boxes of inherited items from a loved one that you've not yet tackled. These areas are tough emotionally, which is the very reason they are still a work in progress.

As the guided journey through your home – room by room – unfolds in this book, you may think that the order in which we suggest you navigate your way through your home is sporadic, and it's very likely your natural inclination will be to want to tackle things in a different way.

However, our decluttering muscle needs to develop one room at a time, so it is sufficiently flexed when we get to the tough stuff. In the same way we wouldn't enter a marathon on our first day of running, so too must we beware of tackling the tough stuff in our homes before we are sufficiently ready. The ultimate aim is that our decluttering muscle is strong enough to facilitate making confident and controlled decisions about what we choose to have in our homes on an ongoing basis.

Therefore, there are going to be things that we are going to ask you to hold off from tackling until later in the project. Sentimental items, for example, will be scattered throughout your home and are difficult to work through early in your journey, so keep these to one side and tackle them after all other rooms in your home are complete. By the time you reach Chapter 12, which focuses on sentimental items, you'll have all the tools you need for success when it comes to approaching them.

When we think about clutter, we don't automatically picture the brandy glass that's been hiding at the back of the kitchen cupboard, the shampoo bottle that is congealed or the duvet set that doesn't fit your current bed. These things are much easier to declutter. They tend to be practical rather than sentimental, and that's the very reason we begin the decluttering journey in rooms that house fewer items that fall into the emotional category. Each room does still have its own related emotions and habits, but these are markedly easier to deal with in the earlier rooms we visit.

If in doubt, don't throw it out

As you work through the rooms in your home, we will be encouraging you to step a little outside your comfort zone. This will open up the possibility of evaluating your items with a fresh perspective.

If you are struggling to make a decision about something, keep it. Yes, we actually said that. If in doubt, don't throw it out. It's important that you feel fully in control of each and every choice you make. If you let go of something you weren't ready for, you will second-guess yourself and feel resentful of and unnerved by the process.

You need to allow yourself the time and space to make gradual progress and feel confident your decisions are the right ones for you today. In fact, we urge you to reframe your decluttering so your main focus is on making a decision about what to *keep* rather than what to let go. Just that simple switch in perspective can be powerful.

Do understand the power of planning

In the same way that every decluttering transformation needs a goal, it also needs a plan. This is key to the decluttering and organising process. Planning comes in different forms, which we'll explain in brief here and then expand upon as we move through each chapter.

TAKE PHOTOS AND VIDEOS

Take some time to think about where you are now. Document your very own 'before'. It can seem like the last thing you want to do if you feel embarrassed or disappointed by what your home looks like today, but trust us, seeing your project progress in visual or written form is one of the biggest motivators out there.

It's not just about pictures, either. Jot down what you are thinking, what you are feeling and what are you hoping for, even if you don't really want to. You'll thank us later when you encounter bumps in the road and need to take the time to remind yourself just how far you've come.

Keep these photos and notes to one side until you've started to make inroads into your clutter and pull them out when you need a boost. We'll be reminding you at the start and end of each room to chronicle your journey.

GIVE DECLUTTERING THE ATTENTION IT DESERVES

The last thing you need when you are in full flow of decluttering decision-making is to be taken off track, so minimise distractions by turning off notifications on your phone. Only take calls if you really have to. Let people in your home know that you mean business and don't want to be disturbed. Treat each decluttering session as if you were in a work meeting and give it the time and focus that will lead to success.

PREPARE YOUR SPACE

Putting in some time to prepare your space is vital too. In each room we tackle, we are going to give you practical advice on how you can set yourself up for success. Decluttering a kitchen involves a very different approach to decluttering a garage, for example. We'll provide hints and tips galore to help you work through each room in a controlled manner using the same methodology we use every day as professional organisers. This includes choosing which bin bags to use, opening curtains and windows, and having cleaning products to hand. These are simple but impactful tweaks and will make all the difference to your success.

Do understand the impact of timing

Timing is everything when it comes to decluttering your home. Think back to your past experiences of embarking on a decluttering project. Did you overstretch yourself, get worn out and give up? If so, you're not on your own. So, let's remedy that.

EVALUATE YOUR INTERNAL CLOCK

Ask yourself if you are a morning, afternoon or evening person. Do you do your best work as soon as you've woken up or do you have more energy and time in the evening? Do you take medication that means you often get off to a slow start? Maybe you don't have the slightest chance of making progress during your working week and your decluttering efforts need to be scheduled at the weekend or during the holidays when you have support. Treat your decluttering time as an appointment like any other work or home commitment, otherwise it will never get to the top of your to-do list.

USE A TIMER

Think too about how long you can normally work before you start to flag. For example, perhaps you'd like to schedule breaks before you begin. Timers work particularly well in the decluttering world to help you stay on track with rest periods.

You see, lots of people make the mistake of starting to declutter and then not stopping until hours later. By then, they are dehydrated, hungry and completely shattered, and they collapse on the sofa, exhausted by the process. Overstretching yourself in this way can then put you off, and ultimately lead to unfinished decluttering projects. By contrast, taking regular breaks to drink, eat and recharge will allow you to make a value judgement about whether you want to go back for more today, tomorrow or next week; taking breaks will keep the momentum going.

Do set goals

In all the years we have been working as professional organisers, the one thing that always surprises the people we work with is our obsession with goals. Now, 'obsession' sounds a tad dramatic, but if we're being honest, we do think goals are absolutely critical. Show us a successful transformational journey where there wasn't a solid goal at its core? Decluttering and organising your home is no different.

And when setting goals, it's important to be clear about how they work.

WORK OUT YOUR BIG-PICTURE GOAL FOR EACH ROOM

The big-picture goal is vital and revolves around determining what your *why* is. Questions to think about to help you define your big-picture goals could be:

- Why exactly is decluttering now at the top of your agenda?
- Why are you continuing to devote attention to decluttering and what will the light at the end of the tunnel look like for you?
- Can you visualise what you'd like your space to look like?
- How is your life going to be different after your successful decluttering journey?
- What possibilities will open up for you if you no longer need to spend as much time and effort at home sorting and tidying?

These bigger goals then help you sustain motivation and momentum as you navigate your way through your home. We will encourage you to have an overarching goal for each area you work on.

Don't do too much at once

As you tackle each room in your home in the upcoming chapters, we are going to urge you to break down your big-picture goal into many smaller, manageable sections within each room. One drawer at a time, one cupboard at a time, one shelf at a time, one pile at a time. By doing so, slowly but surely the clutter will start to disappear and the order will start to reappear.

Do invest time in gathering like with like

When you are decluttering, organising and categorising your home, we will urge you to gather 'like with like', but what does that actually mean? In very simple terms, it's literally the process of gathering similar items together, for example gathering all your socks together, all your pillowcases together, all your recipe books together.

As we amass more items in our homes, we begin to lose track of what we actually have as things may have become scattered across different rooms or different drawers and shelves. But in order to make sensible decisions about what we are going to keep, we need to have the full picture of what is actually in our homes, and gathering like with like helps with this.

When all items from the same category are together it is much easier for us to make an assessment of whether we have a sensible amount of an item or way too many for our needs, and it's also helpful in assessing our storage needs too. Confronting ourselves with the true, full picture of what we have is a very powerful technique that is going to be pivotal to our success.

Don't rush out to buy storage

When thinking about decluttering, you can be forgiven for having a vision in your mind of a perfectly curated room, for example a kitchen with labelled glass jars and rotating Perspex bottle holders. But we want to issue one word of caution when it comes to decluttering and storage: Wait!

The time for sourcing storage solutions is late into the decluttering process, and considering storage is one of the last things we do in each room.

Don't make the mistake of buying storage too early and favouring form over function. Decluttering must come first so you know what exactly it is that you need to store, and therefore what storage you need to buy in terms of volume, size, practicality and manageability, to name but a few considerations.

The chances are, too, that you may already have adequate storage in your home, once you've pared everything back. (The one thing that cluttered homes are often not short of is storage solutions!)

So, our advice is to tap into temporary storage solutions for now: old cardboard boxes, shoe boxes and takeaway containers are all great until you understand what you really need. As you work through your decluttering, organising and categorising, using temporary storage will allow you the time to consider whether open or closed boxes are going to work for you, for example, and, as you near the end of the process, you'll be able to find the perfect solution that makes storing and finding things in your home a breeze.

Do consider where your decluttered stuff will go

When you're getting ready to declutter you need to plan in advance where all the things you no longer need or want are going. The last thing you want is to have bags and bags of stuff you keep tripping over in your hallway or riding around in the boot of your car forever and a day. Getting your unwanted items out of your home and to their next destination is a vital component of your decluttering.

KEEP THINGS SIMPLE

Our main advice? Keep things simple. If you can donate to a charity or thrift store, find one that isn't overly discerning about what they will or won't accept. Make a phone call in advance so there are no surprises when you arrive with your donations. If possible, choose a charity shop that accepts donations all day every day and where parking or travel there is straightforward.

Just remember, the main goal is to keep focusing on decluttering progress rather than finding the perfect charity for every item. We want you to succeed and don't want to see any barriers standing in your way.

DO YOUR RESEARCH

Where you live will dictate your options for disposing of your decluttered items, but once you have spent some time doing your research, possibilities may open up that you had never considered before.

Make a point of familiarising yourself with your local tip or recycling centre. If you know what recycling options are available, you can ensure you sort as you go to minimise the toing and froing when you get there.

For those items that could be reused but are not well suited to charity shops, such as food, individual stationery items and DIY items, there are lots of options. You can give away items via apps, local Facebook groups and food banks.

If you don't have transport to take your unwanted items to the recycling centre or charity shop, be sure to research other options. For example, you could ask a friend to help you transport your items, you could find a charity shop that collects items from your home, or you could consider hiring a van. Get all of this organised in good time.

DON'T PUT A BURDEN ON OTHER PEOPLE

If you are going to give your stuff to a friend or family member, make sure in advance that they definitely want it. Often we try to pass on our unwanted things to friends because we are trying to alleviate our own guilt in letting go of things. Some people may not want your stuff but are too polite to say no when you offer. That said, once you've had the conversation and agreed they do want them, it's nice to see your things being reused and enjoyed by someone else.

VALUE YOUR TIME WHEN SELLING

If an item has value, you might consider selling it on sites such as eBay, Vinted or Facebook Marketplace. Before deciding to sell, you need to do your research and see if it is worth your time and effort. The last thing you want is to create a whole room of stuff you want to sell and then never get around to it. We want you to succeed in your decluttering and often keeping stuff to one side for selling is the barrier that stops that from happening.

Don't be distracted by other people and their stuff

A word of warning: now's not the time to start directing your decluttering attention to other people's stuff! When your side of the wardrobe is perfectly curated and all you see is the chaos on the other side, it can be super frustrating. But it's important to recognise this stage of the decluttering process as your individual journey.

Not everyone in your world will be motivated to declutter to the same degree within the same timescales. (In fact, other people in your household may even doubt your ability to make progress or may interfere in your decision-making.) Our advice is to stick to your lane, stick to your stuff, and ignore the back-seat drivers.

What often happens is that other people in your household will slowly but surely start to see the results of your hard work. They will see your stress start to dissipate, the household expenditure decrease and the calm start to ascend. That's when they get interested in decluttering. So, be patient. If you build it, they will come – or we hope so anyway!

TAKE A MOMENT

Now we've whizzed through a mini decluttering 101, we suggest you take five minutes to think about whether you have followed (or fallen foul of!) some of these dos and don'ts of decluttering in the past. To help with this, consider the following:

- Have you felt aggrieved that people with bigger homes have it easier?
- Have you factored in the reality of your physical and mental health?
- Have you thought about your big-picture goals and ensured that you can break each goal down into an achievable action?
- Have you taken the time to plan how your decluttering session will look?
- Have you thought about where your decluttered items will go?
- Have you worked out when you are likely to get the best out of yourself?
- Have you run out to buy new storage before you even know what needs to be stored?

4

The kitchen

'What's more important – the space or the stuff?'

A kitchen reigns supreme as the primary hub of the home. As such, it's a heavy-use part of any household and the average kitchen holds thousands of items in it. Yet the kitchen will be the very first project on our decluttering journey. Why is this?

Well, we begin in the kitchen because this is a room full of mainly functional items. This means that even though we do have a connection to our stuff in there, it's mostly on a practical level and we should be faced with lots of **no-brainer decisions**. Therefore, in the kitchen, very basic decluttering questions – Do I need it?, Do I use it? and Do I love it? – should serve you well and see you through 80 per cent of the decisions needed in the room. Very few items in the kitchen need to be analysed at a deeper emotional level than this. (Although, of course, when those decisions do crop up, as they will in every room of your home, we'll make sure you're armed and ready!) So, at face value, a decluttering project in the kitchen should be easy(ish) to navigate emotionally, so that's where we choose to start.

JARGON BUSTER

No-brainer decision – a decision to declutter something that should be obvious, quick and require little to no soul-searching.

That being said, there's no denying that the kitchen is a tough room to declutter logistically. Every fork, every tin opener, every stock cube, every tin of tuna lays claim to space in your kitchen. Each and every one of these items needs to be managed: taken out of the cupboard for cleaning, a decision made and then put back into the right cupboard. Every single item needs to justify its spot, and so a lot of different choices have to be made.

Even though making a decision about whether to keep three or four flavours of the five herbal teas that you have in your tea cupboard may seem unimportant, it's this granular level of decision-making that is going to make all the difference to your success, so be sure to give it the time and thought it deserves, which requires time and energy. Remember, this room is the first one you are tackling, so you may struggle at times. Focus on the progress you are making though, rather than what you find tricky, and it will serve you well. Rome wasn't built in a day and neither will a perfectly configured, clutter-free kitchen be.

The chances are that you'll need to prepare food in your kitchen on decluttering day too, so you'll have to take it slowly and manage your time well, allowing for people to make use of the room as you work. If you don't do this then your stress levels will rise, and you'll ditch the project and fall at the first hurdle (and we definitely don't want that!).

If your difficulty with decluttering in the past has come from a struggle to make the right choices, then you might be feeling a bit nervous right now about the number of decisions required in the kitchen, but please don't worry. This book is all about giving you the skills you need to make those decisions much more easily. We'll begin with the thinking first by digging into the emotions and habits that crop up for us in the kitchen, and then move into the doing stage forewarned and forearmed. Let's get started.

The thinking

Emotional Preparation

One of the most important things to be mindful of is that decluttering is never about the stuff; the thing that holds us back is our emotional connection to the stuff. So by thinking about the emotions and habits that often present themselves in a kitchen first, we'll be more mindful and thorough when we embark on the doing. Let's go through them.

SAVVY SHOPPING

Sometimes the excess of food we find in our kitchens is quite simply the culmination of years of engrained shopping habits. Food shopping is something most of us do at least once a week and we become entrenched in our habits. We always do what we have always done.

If we have always done a 'big shop' each week, for example, we continue to do so, often without question. If you are doing your weekly food shop online, do you always default to adding your 'favourites' to your cart out of habit? Or when you pop to the shops, do you throw your regular items into your bag without knowing for certain whether you already have them at home?

Let's face it, we find ourselves overrun with clutter because we buy stuff, often too much stuff. But who is to blame? Well, mostly we are, but on occasion we can be forgiven because there are some very clever marketing minds at work conspiring against us to make us just … buy … one … more. So, are you a marketer's dream come true?

Do you struggle to walk past special offer sections in the supermarket without picking something up, and if it's on a three-for-two offer can you just not resist? Do you buy things with a very short shelf life because they are marked down? If you're at the 'Before you go – you may like this' section in your online shopping order do you always take a sneaky peak? They know just how to draw us in, don't they?

Bulk-buying is something to consider here too. There's no doubt that bulk-buying can be of financial benefit, and who are we to question if it makes sense to bulk-buy certain things? We all have to determine for ourselves what is more important to us: saving money or saving space. When it comes to bulk-buying, it's all about compromise. But all we're saying is that a 48-pack of loo rolls doesn't enhance the look at the top of your fridge freezer. So, if it's clutter-free living you're after, altering your bulk-buying habits needs to be on your hit list.

All in all, it's vital to challenge your own shopping behaviours at this stage so you can gradually become more aware of the habits that are holding you back from having a clutter-free home. We suggest you take a list to the shops and stick to it. That special deal will still be there next week (or one just like it!), so only buy it if you actually need it.

ACKNOWLEDGE ASPIRATIONS

Aspiration is a big emotion when it comes to kitchens. We've just talked about how we sometimes get stuck in a rut and continue to buy the same things over and over, but other times we get fed up and want to make changes. (Do you see how complex clutter is? It gets you both ways.)

Food

So what do we mean when it comes to aspirational food? Here are some examples:

- You read online about a new superfood that's guaranteed to make you healthier, less bloated and sleep better. But you buy it, eat it once, forget about it, and then the rest of it sits in your cupboard for months.
- Perhaps it's the summer holidays so you plan a bake day with your kids. You use what's needed for the recipe but that multipack of rainbow writing icing lies unloved and untouched in your cupboard for years. This goes on until you do your next bake day but, of course, you forget what you have and go out and buy a whole new pack.
- You see a recipe that needs saffron, pay a fortune for it, use a strand, and never cook that recipe again.
- You plan to save money on your food bill so you buy a 'value' version of a tinned item to try. But you don't like the taste and revert to your old favourite instead. You're then left with three of the four-pack of tins taking up valuable space in your cupboard.

We'll stop there, but the list is endless…

Gadgets

Spiralisers, mandolins, bread makers, strawberry hullers, chopsticks, coffee grinders – I could go on but you get the drift. Aspirational gadgets can take up a lot of space.

It may be that you swear by your coffee grinder (and lots of people do), but we'd wager that there are far more people with a coffee grinder in their kitchen who don't use it than do. And that's the point. We all have things in our homes that we aspire to use, that felt like a great idea at the time when we bought them. But now, in our current, daily lives, they are taking up valuable space *and* making us feel guilty about the money we spent on them.

Your job is to try and work out what your own version of a strawberry huller* is and then decide whether it's actually useful to you or whether it's simply crammed into a cupboard making your bog-standard but heavily used cheese grater impossible to get to.

(*If you are scratching your head and wondering what a strawberry huller is then you're not alone. It's a gadget to take out strawberry stalks. Yep, that's actually a thing!)

The look

And finally, there are things that *look* aspirational that could be standing in your way. It's lovely to have that cornflower blue Kitchen Aid or top-of-the-range Gaggia out on your work surface, but are you actually making use of them? Now, we've got nothing against beautiful kitchen appliances – we've got some, too – but if you can see a layer of dust on them then maybe it's time to question the space they are taking up on your work surface and in your life.

And we can't not mention those beautifully labelled jars. Decanting food and other kitchen items into jars can be a brilliant way to manage your kitchen, but it's quite the undertaking to keep up with the system. The key here is to recognise whether it is going to be a help or a hindrance in your life. There's no point curating an **Insta-perfect** jar selection if you can't find your baked beans.

JARGON BUSTER

Insta-perfect – an unobtainable, stylised representation of a room that does not reflect real life and serves only to make us feel inadequate on social media.

TACKLING TRANSITIONS

Our lives ebb and flow, and each of life's transitions can bring with it changes to the way we work in our kitchens, from changes to the food we cook to changes to the tools we need. Let's dig into this further.

Life stages can look like any of the following: living life as a student in a shared house; living alone for the first time; moving in with a partner and amalgamating two homes; expanding your family with one, two, three, four, five … kids; adjusting to being an empty nester; or downsizing to a smaller property. These stages of life may feel familiar to you and you may have experienced many of them, or perhaps just one or two. But one of these stages will undoubtedly feel like a very special period in your life and if that period of fond memories and fun times has now passed, it can be difficult to move on easily.

For example, if you have always loved cooking for your family then it can be a tough wrench to see your children fly the nest and no longer eat with you regularly. Often it takes time to adjust, even on a practical level, such as remembering to get the portions right cooking for only two when you've been used to cooking for five people.

Or, when embarking on parenthood, very little can prepare us for the reality of what awaits. The Instagram version of life with a baby shows a parent feeding their baby quietly in a clutter-free, serene room. But the realistic version is wall-to-wall plastic bottles, sterilisers and washing up on the side because you've had no sleep and no time to do it. Babies and kids need stuff, so in your kitchen you need to make room for it all. Now, that's a transition to beat all transitions.

As a result of life's transitions, there are hard but necessary questions we need to ask ourselves as we navigate the world of clutter. Are you clinging on to the memory of a period of your life that no longer exists? How big is your household now? How often do you entertain in reality? All of these changes can affect simple things such as how many mugs you have in your cupboard or how much food you need to buy at the supermarket. So, whether the number of people in your household is on an upwards or downwards trajectory, it's important to keep on top of these changes so that clutter doesn't take over.

SORTING OUT SENTIMENTAL

Sentimentality is everywhere in our homes. And rightly so. It's important to preserve memories of special times in our lives. And although there are fewer sentimental items in the kitchen compared to other areas of our homes, the kitchen doesn't escape sentimentality completely.

This is because the items in our kitchens have often been used over and over throughout the years and therefore form a vivid part of our memories. That might be the novelty mug your late dad drank out of every day; the dinner set brought out for special celebrations when you were a child; or the chopsticks you brought back from your travels in your twenties. All these things evoke a special memory and add a different dimension to the things in our kitchens.

Yet kitchen space is **prime real estate** and needs to be well utilised. Not many people have a sprawling kitchen with ample space, so we have to make careful choices. Every sentimental item we store means one less space for a functional item we use every day, so we need to establish a sentimental item's true value to us. We need to seek out the quality over the quantity to facilitate a harmonious balance between practical and sentimental.

JARGON BUSTER

Prime real estate – an area in your home that makes a huge difference to the functionality of your day-to-day life and consequently needs careful management.

TAKE A MOMENT

So, let's pause and assess which of the topics discussed in this 'emotional preparation' section have been holding you back from keeping your kitchen clutter-free. It may be one or two of them, or it may be a combination of them all.

Before we move on, take some time to consider the following:

- Do you simply go through the motions when it comes to your regular food shop? Are you a sucker for a sale?
- Is **shiny object syndrome** causing you problems? Are you always succumbing to the latest fad?
- Has your life moved into a new era but you've not caught up emotionally just yet?
- Are you so attached to things from days gone by that you struggle to fit regular, everyday stuff in your cupboard?

JARGON BUSTER

Shiny object syndrome – a continual state of distraction by the next new big thing. To be avoided at all costs.

Goal Setting

Now we've done the emotional preparation, it's time to set some goals for the kitchen.

BIG-PICTURE GOALS

We explained the importance of assigning a big-picture goal to every decluttering project you undertake back on p. 35, so here's your first opportunity to think about what yours might be in your kitchen.

Below are some examples for you to ponder, but this is far from an exhaustive list:

- You want to save money by being able to see more clearly what you have, so you can avoid buying duplicates.
- You want to make cooking more pleasurable by having a clear work surface.
- You want to save time by being able to easily put things away after dinner.
- You want to save your sanity by making sure everyone in the house knows where things belong.
- You want to enjoy spending time with friends in your kitchen without feeling embarrassed.

Determining your big-picture goal at this stage is vital, so even though you're chomping at the bit to get started, take five minutes to think about what it is that is going to keep your momentum going. Write it down and keep it front of mind.

Planning Section by Section

When you have your big-picture goal in place, it's time to consider working in smaller sections of the kitchen. If you aim to do whole rooms in one day, you may burn out and lose momentum before you've even got off the starting blocks. It is therefore imperative to break every room down into manageable sections and have smaller goals for each decluttering session you undergo, whether that's a 10-minute burst or a four-hour commitment. The good news is that our kitchens already have clearly defined sections as they will be split into cupboards, drawers and shelves, so planning how you will work section by section is more straightforward here than in other rooms of your home.

We suggest splitting your kitchen into food and non-food sections. Here's a list of suggested categories in each to allow you to plan.

FOOD CATEGORIES
- Canned and tinned goods
- Pasta, rice, noodles and pulses
- Herbs and spices

- Oils, vinegars, sauces and condiments
- Drinks
- Snacks
- Tea, coffee and milk drinks
- Cereals
- Baking goods

NON-FOOD CATEGORIES

- Glasses
- Mugs and cups
- Flasks and water bottles
- Tableware
- Serving dishes
- Cutlery and knives
- Utensils
- Preparation gadgets
- Storage containers
- Pots and pans
- Bakeware
- Electrical appliances
- Foils and plastics
- Cleaning products
- Carrier bags
- Junk drawer
- Recipe books
- Kitchen counter
- Table linen
- Vases and flowerpots

Take a look around your kitchen to assess how you are going to break it down. Will you be able to do all your food cupboards in one day or is that too ambitious? Just how extensive is your kitchen equipment? How quickly will the kitchen need to become usable again? Do you have cupboards that you already know will contain some easy wins? Giving yourself time to assess the practicalities of breaking this room down is truly going to reap rewards.

One quick caveat. It's important to focus your attention on the insides of cupboards and drawers at this early stage. While the clutter on your kitchen work surfaces may be what grinds you down, you need to tackle what's inside first to allow space to open up for you to relocate things that have been on countertops back into cupboards later if you want to.

PHYSICAL PREPARATION AND LOGISTICS

The final stage of preparation is all about the logistics, so it's time to do the following:

Decide what surface you are going to use to put the items you take out of cupboards on to. Do you have a kitchen table or a clear work surface, perhaps? Or is your floor clean enough and clear enough to work on? A floor is ideal for sorting out things from your base units as it helps logistically, but you need to be physically able to sit and twist. Working from the floor will save you time and energy but it's not for everyone. Next best is a work surface, purely because of its proximity to the cupboards, but it needs to be clear. Can you move anything from your work surface to a table to facilitate your project? You'll be surprised by just how much comes out of each cupboard once you start working.

Pull your outdoor recycling bins as close to the house as possible so you have easy access to them for food that is out of date and needs to be discarded. Be mindful that it can take some time to empty the tins or jars, dispose of the contents, and then wash and recycle the containers correctly.

Gather your cleaning supplies. Make sure you have plenty of hot water, an abundance of cleaning and drying cloths and whatever your cleaning product of choice is to hand. Kitchens get dirty and we'll be cleaning as we go, one area at a time.

Think of your exit plan. Is there a nearby charity or food bank that you can donate things to easily? Ensure you have boxes to hand to store anything you want to give away. Boxes work well for both food and non-food items, but the destination is likely to be different for each so we suggest that you store them separately as you go. Bin bags don't work as well for kitchen non-food items, whereas sturdy cardboard boxes are perfect.

Grab a box or large bag. Things that you'll find in the kitchen that belong elsewhere in the house need to be moved and you'll need a sturdy bag or box to do this.

Take some 'before' photos to look back on later (even though this may be the last thing you want to do right now!).

Now we've done the thinking, it time to start flexing that decluttering muscle. Ready?

The doing

How and Where to Get Started

It's important to take things one cupboard and one drawer at a time. The kitchen is in constant use, so you can't drag every pot, pan, glass and bag of pasta out of every cupboard all at once and hope for the best. People might be popping in and out for a cup of tea, to make a sandwich or to grab a snack and you need to make sure they are not breaking their neck (and your things) doing so.

It may make sense to tackle things literally one cupboard or one category at a time, or you may want to tackle your kitchen in stages – maybe all the food at once, all the lower cupboards and drawers or all the random places, such as the junk drawers, work surfaces and fridge fronts, together.

Every kitchen is completely different, so take the time to evaluate what makes sense given the parameters of yours; the order in which you tackle it is down to you. If necessary, use a checklist to keep you on track with what's been done and what hasn't. Even though it may seem obvious, it's good to keep a record of your progress.

GATHER LIKE WITH LIKE

When you have chosen an area to start with, gather, gather, gather until you have everything from the category you are working on together. And we mean *everything*. Why? So you can evaluate your numbers. Only when you have a full picture of what you have can you make a decision about which ones are most valuable to you, which ones are in better shape and, most importantly, confront yourself with where you have excess.

If you're tackling your drinks cupboard, pull those bottles of wine down from the top of your fridge and put them next to the ones you keep in your cupboard. When you're tackling your glasses, put the tumblers from the cupboard next to those oversized wine glasses that have to go in with the cereals because they are too tall for your shelf. Gather those utensils from the utensils drawer, from the cutlery drawer and from the jar on top of your work surface and put them all together. Grab those water bottles from every backpack, every bedroom and those that are right at the back of that pesky corner cupboard you loathe. Rescue the cleaning products from under your sink, in your utility room, in your garage and in your bathrooms. Empty your dishwasher, do the washing up and bring everything together in one place.

Remember to work one category or one section at a time so you don't get overwhelmed, but for each category you need to make sure you have everything available to you.

Now we've gathered everything together there will undoubtedly be decisions that are straightforward, so let's kick off with some easy wins.

Decluttering Category by Category

EASY WINS

Food that is way out of date. Whether or not you choose to still consume things that are past their sell-by date is a personal decision but ask yourself why it's still there after so long.

Plastic straws. We bought a hundred of them for a kid's party five years ago and the last 70 are still sitting waiting to be used. Is it ever going to happen? Let them go.

Old dish cloths with holes. Life's too short. Give your cleaning equipment a fighting chance of doing a decent job.

Tombola or raffle prizes. There's a reason the person decided to give them to the tombola and it's rarely because it's their favourite tipple. Let them go!

Things waiting to be recycled from your junk drawer. Make a point of recycling those old batteries and bulbs and free up some space.

Chopsticks. If eating Asian food is a once-a-year pastime, a knife and fork will be just fine if you're tight on space.

DIG DEEPER

For less obvious decisions in the kitchen it's time to return to the emotions we talked about on p. 42, so we can challenge items that we have doubts about. Remember to make your decisions one item at a time and stay fully in control of what's staying and what's going.

Food

Food is tricky because it 'could' always be used. But will it? That's the question. And more importantly, how much space, time and energy is being taken up by it simply being there? The aim here is realism. This is about seeking out those things in your food cupboards in date that *will* be used and then also making a sensible plan about the *could* be used category, so that it can be switched into a 'will'. You can do this one of two ways: inventive meal planning or donating.

You can bet your bottom dollar there will be someone out there who loves a piece of *stollen* with their coffee, so you won't have to search long before finding willing and grateful takers for your donations. And what's not to love about a random dinner with bulgur wheat to start and *stollen* for dessert? How you choose to work through the excess food in your kitchen is your choice to make. The main thing is it doesn't sit there for another three years untouched and unnoticed.

Glasses

In order to ascertain how many glasses is the right amount for your household, think about your preferences. What type of glass do you gravitate towards? Have your drinking habits changed, especially when it comes to the types of glasses available for all the different types of alcohol? There's no need for you to have six sherry schooners if you haven't touched sherry since the 1990s. Evaluate your space, preferences and habits and pare down glassware to a sensible amount.

Mugs and cups

Mugs and cups are a popular choice when it comes to gifts from other people, so it's likely you will have gifts you love and others you've never used. Don't be afraid to offload sentimental mugs if they are taking up valuable space that would make your everyday mugs and cups more easily accessible. (Or put these sentimental mugs aside for now to deal with later, in Chapter 12.)

Flasks and water bottles

When it comes to flasks and water bottles, the quality will dictate the likelihood of you using them. If a flask doesn't keep drinks warm or a water bottle doesn't keep things cold, it's likely that you'll subconsciously never choose it. Accept that you will have inevitably bought an occasional substandard product over the years, let it go and move on.

Tableware

What is it about that plate that means it never sees the light of day? Too big for the cupboard? Too heavy to wash up? Not part of a matching set? Chipped or cracked? You don't need to keep every plate you have ever owned. Choose a sensible amount and let some go.

Serving dishes

Serving dishes are often things that are passed down through generations. Are the ones you have fit for purpose or have you replaced them with more modern versions? Do they stack easily or are they threatening to topple over every time you open the cupboard door? Do you use serving dishes regularly or just on special occasions? Asking these types of question will allow you to evaluate whether the space that serving dishes need is justified.

Cutlery and knives

We have a habit of emptying our cutlery drawers, cleaning them out and just putting everything back. But cutlery and knives need to be assessed just like everything else in the kitchen. Blunt knives, flimsy forks and rusty spoons can be frustrating to use.

Utensils

Where do we even start when it comes to utensils? We're going to keep it simple. If you're anything like the majority of the population, you probably have way too many, so really assess whether you have an alternative option that can do the same job. There's a reason why utensil drawers are constantly jamming! They're chock-full of aspirational items used on an infrequent basis. So, be strong and let those duplicate utensils go!

Preparation gadgets

Preparation gadgets like cheese graters, measuring bowls and measuring jugs are similar to utensils. We can often live with a simple collection of everyday items, so be selective when deciding what to keep.

Storage containers

Plastic containers come in from many sources so your numbers will increase regularly. Be realistic about how many you need. Are you batch cooking, or taking lunches to work or school? How much space do you have to store them? All these things will have a bearing on the decisions you make when working through your plastic containers. The issue of how storage containers become separated on what seems like a weekly basis from their lids will remain one of life's mysteries till the end of time, but if you simply cannot locate their partner, do yourself a favour and let them go.

Pots and pans

You've only got so many rings on your hob and so much space in your oven, so if you have five times as many pots and pans as you could realistically use, it's time to look at the reality of your cooking habits. Are your pans fit for purpose, still non-stick, not too heavy, no loose handles? All these things create a psychological barrier to you using them so be sure to make sensible decisions.

Bakeware

The amount of bakeware you need will be governed by whether or not you are a baker. The problem with baking equipment is that we rarely make a decision to let it go, because we think that it will be used one day. Realism is everything here. Bakeware can be cumbersome to store and therefore needs to justify its space in kitchen cupboards.

Electrical appliances

Electrical appliances and gadgets are actually quite simple to evaluate. They are either in use regularly or aspirational. It all boils down to whether you need the space or the stuff more. The reason why this feels so hard is because it almost seems like you are admitting failure. As if you had a great idea for improvement and it didn't quite pan out and now you are left with the stuff to remind you of what you didn't do.

Cleaning products

Often the biggest contributor to clutter in a kitchen is ironically the very thing that we purchase to help us. We buy the latest cleaning product in the vain hope that it will fill a void in our cleaning process but one squirt and no miracle fix means the product is consigned to the darkest depths of an under-sink cupboard for years with lots of friends. Be realistic, be ruthless and be rid.

There are other categories in a kitchen – beyond the list above – not to miss, too. Look at your carrier bags, your recipe books, your table linen and your vases and flowerpots, for example. We often omit them from our decluttering schedules but letting the excess go can be a huge space saver.

Reframe Your Thinking

ACKNOWLEDGE ASPIRATIONS

See letting go of that spiraliser as a move towards embracing a simpler way of meal preparation. When you donate that baking equipment, remind yourself you are learning to understand what enhances your current life. When you ditch that sushi mat, think about the fact that you get way more joy from eating the sushi than painstakingly rolling it. It's tough to move past aspirational thinking, but once you are armed with more self-awareness, you'll be so much less likely to succumb to shiny object syndrome in the future.

TACKLING TRANSITIONS

When it comes to tackling transitions, it is about – to all intents and purposes – evaluating where we are in life, so dig deep and embrace honesty. If the size of your household is increasing, you need to get acquainted with compromise, and if your household size is decreasing, it's time for a reality check. But either way, it's a case of out with the old to make space for the new. Transition, regeneration and evolution is a part of life that should be enjoyed, not feared, and this is the time to get honest with yourself and make sure your things reflect the current you.

Should those souvenir shot glasses from your twenties stay while you desperately need space for your children's water bottles? Do you need to have a 72-piece dinner service when you generally cook for two and go to your daughter's every Christmas? Don't allow your cupboards to house things that you don't use and mean that you struggle to find and store the things that you do.

Organising the Things we Are Letting go of

We need to deal with the things that don't belong in your kitchen during this part of the project. This might be moving items you found in the kitchen (such as clothing or books, for example) into a bag or box to put into the bedroom or study later, so the items can be returned to the part of the house to which they belong. It might be gathering sentimental items together and putting them aside to tackle further down the line, in Chapter 12. Then, of course, we need to make sure we have the items we have decided to let go of in clearly defined bags or boxes in line with the exit plan for decluttered kitchen items that we planned on p. 51.

A couple of caveats:

- **No maybe boxes allowed.** If you are not comfortable letting an item go at this stage then it should stay. Putting an item on the backburner for another day by moving it somewhere else is not going to make that decision easier, so keep it where you can see it in the kitchen, so you have the opportunity to evaluate it while you are going about your day-to-day kitchen business.
- **No flitting.** If you are prone to getting sidetracked when you go elsewhere, don't leave the room. Just put the items that need to be relocated somewhere to the side so you can tackle them later, once you have completed this round of your kitchen project.

Organising the Things we Are Keeping

And now we have dealt with the things we don't need in the kitchen, it's time to work with the things we do. It's time to start putting things back, which can feel like a game of *Tetris*!

Work out which cupboard or drawer best suits the stuff you are working with, grab your storage container if relevant (you can use temporary storage for the time being, until you've decided what permanent storage works for you) and move things into their new home.

But should they have a new home, you ask? Well, if the home they have works, leave them where they are but think about the things that are not working. Think about whether you have any of the following:

- barriers that stop you putting that item away;
- areas of your kitchen that you find tricky to access;
- trips you are making back and forth across your kitchen for items you are using regularly.

Evaluate what's working and what's not and be open to change.

When it comes to where to put things in a kitchen it boils down to three things: logic, accessibility and compromise.

1. LOGIC

Logic is an interesting one because we all have brains that work in completely different ways. What is logical to one person may not be logical to another. The beauty of home organisation is that you can create a system that's unique to you and your household. There is not a one-size-fits-all solution. And you need to search for yours. For example, who are we to say that baking equipment needs to go higher up in your kitchen because it is used less frequently, when you might be a master baker?

Exercising logic is all about asking yourself where you would naturally go looking for something. What would it be near? Ask your family for advice if they are heavy users of the kitchen. A logical solution needs to work for everyone otherwise you're going to be the one constantly putting things in their rightful place. And don't be scared to move things around in a kitchen. It might take 27 attempts at looking for your mugs in the place they've always been, but soon enough your subconscious brain will shift into gear and send you to their new, more accessible, more logical location. Moving the location of things in the kitchen is annoying in the short term but worth it in the long run, if it works better.

This kitchen project is going to evolve. You may find you allocate a home for something early in the process and then change its location later once you start to see the full picture. Having said that, if it ain't broke, don't fix it. If something works in a certain drawer, then leave it there. It's the things that are awkward, that have you wasting a valuable five seconds here, ten seconds there that we need to look at.

2. ACCESSIBILITY

Accessibility is critical, as speed and ease of use of everyday items in the kitchen is key. Put the things you use most frequently, such as tea, coffee and mugs, at eye level. Store the infrequently used items on top shelves or in awkward corner cupboards, so here we're talking about party dishes or seasonal dinner services. Don't over stack heavy items, such as pans and crock pots, and ensure you keep them lower down so you safeguard your back and your head.

Think outside the box – for example, move shelves that have always been at an awkward height. If it's going to be better, you may even remove a shelf or add one in. This is your chance to fine-tune things and make your kitchen operate like a dream.

3. COMPROMISE

Sometimes our spaces can't be dreamlike. Sometimes we just don't have all the space we'd like and that's where compromise kicks in. Do the very best you can with the space you have. Space is finite but stuff isn't, so it boils down to a decision about what you want more: the space or the stuff, the stress or the calm, the strawberry huller or the cheese grater? You decide!

Choosing the Right Storage

Hands up if you love to buy storage? And hands up if you're already googling 'boxes' before someone so much as says the word 'declutter'? Well, we have good news and bad. First, the good: we love a container in the kitchen. And now the bad: there's lots to think about before you can hit that 'add to cart' button.

Temporary storage is just fine as we're working through our items and deciding where they should go in our kitchens. Most of us who have become overwhelmed with clutter have plenty of storage boxes hanging around that we can use. Have you looked? Shoe boxes, phone boxes or plastic takeaway containers will work fine until we find the perfect container. Let's use what we have and not add to the volume of stuff in our homes unnecessarily.

But when your decluttering decisions have been made and you are ready to think about storage, we recommend choosing function over form every single time.

If we are going to use a container, it needs to make things easier rather than more difficult. Do you need a lid? Is decanting food into containers after a trip to the supermarket something you will be able to maintain? Is a box made out of fabric going to be durable enough to withstand all the daily life that gets thrown at a kitchen? Does your container make it easier or harder to access things? There's no point in having something that looks the part if it doesn't play the part. It's all too easy to be influenced by the beautiful shots you see on your social media feed but what's the reality behind that photo? What's out of shot? Dig deep to find that realism that's going to make your kitchen declutter such a success. Don't **micro-organise** if you are a **macro-organisation** person.

JARGON BUSTER

Micro-organising – focusing on the details, often to the detriment of the bigger picture. Micro-organising has its place but only when the foundations are in place.

Macro-organising – focusing on the big picture and ensuring everything has a designated home or zone. Macro-organising is the first vital step in creating order.

If making things look nice in your kitchen is part of your goals, though, there's no problem with that, but do think practicality first and foremost. Grab a tape measure and use it. What's the optimum height to make sure you can access things easily and maximise the height, width and depth you have? If you want similar boxes all throughout your kitchen, what's your budget? What will be the best material for your boxes? There are so many questions to ask to get the perfect kitchen storage solution. This is not something to grab on a whim when you are out shopping. You need to shop with all the right information and intention. There's a box for everything – it's just a matter of finding it.

The Finishing Touches

And we now find ourselves almost at the end. Job done? Not quite. We need to make sure the whole project is finished. So what's involved in finishing the kitchen?

LABELLING

Now, if there's one piece of organisational kit we believe *is* worth the investment it's a label maker. There are ones you type on to and there are ones that use Bluetooth and work via your phone on an app. Your budget, your choice. Sticky notes, paper labels, decals, gift tags and a marker pen – all are absolutely fine. The important thing is that you can identify what belongs there. So grab your labels and start sticking.

You can use labels however you like. You can post information on the inside of a cupboard door. You can label a shelf either on the front or on the top. You can also do both so you have all angles covered. One thing's for sure, once you start using a label maker you will label anything that doesn't move. Did I say how much we like labels? Suffice to say they are a game-changer.

A label will be the lovely friend that you can refer to when your kids or your partner say they don't know where something goes. If it's labelled, there's no excuse. A label will help you, too. Let's go back to those thousands of items we have in the kitchen. That's a lot of categories. And if each of those categories has a label then it's going to be so much easier to keep track and put things away.

CLEANING

If you are working through your decluttering one area at a time in the kitchen then make sure you finish off the cleaning. We suggest you clean the shelves or drawers as you work through your kitchen, but now finish off with the inside and outside of the door or drawer front. Leave no stone unturned to make this the best decluttering project you've ever done: thorough and complete.

REMOVING ITEMS THAT DON'T BELONG IN THE KITCHEN

Now's the time to move things to other destinations. That might mean taking decluttered items to the charity shop or recycling and refuse centre. It may be doing a return you need to make to a store. Or it may be moving the items you found in your kitchen that belong elsewhere (such as clothes or books) to the correct room in the home.

The project isn't complete until everything relating to that project is complete. If possible, try to incorporate a trip to a charity shop into your plans for the day. If that's not practical, plan and diarise when you are going to do it. The job isn't finished until all your excess is gone. It's an integral part of the process. If it's still in your house then it's not officially decluttered.

Enjoy

Now it's time to enjoy the fruits of your labour, because having a decluttered, organised kitchen will mean more time, more productivity, more creativity, less waste, less stress and less guilt. These benefits can last a lifetime.

This is the first room on our decluttering journey and we still have hills to climb and lessons to learn. However, the most important thing is that you have made decisions about your things that you feel in control of. They are the right decisions for now. On another day further down the line, with a stronger decluttering muscle, you may be able to make a different decision, but for today, it's time to enjoy your newly decluttered space and to take an 'after' photo that you can be proud of.

If, however, you are feeling stuck and the decisions and logistics in your kitchen have been difficult, don't lose heart and stay stuck. Move forwards to the next room with the knowledge that you can return to your kitchen when your decluttering muscle is stronger. This is a completely normal part of the process.

Think about the donations you have given that will bring pleasure to someone else rather than sitting unseen and unloved at the back of your pan drawer. Think about the fact that you have gone through your kitchen with a fine-tooth comb and left no stock cube unturned. Think about the decisions you have made – sometimes tough ones – and the way you have taken yourself out of your comfort zone to make the right decisions that you deserve. Think about the way you have done this project in a controlled manner, so much so that you feel no sense of panic about what has gone where.

This feeling of accomplishment is what will drive you forwards to your next room. After all, you are smiling every time you walk into your kitchen, and who doesn't want a bit more of that?

TAKE A MOMENT

 Now you can sit down with a nice cup of tea and spend some time evaluating your kitchen project:

- Did you learn anything during the kitchen declutter that will help you in the upcoming rooms?
- Have you found any area of the kitchen more satisfying than another?
- Did you come across any barriers or hurdles you need to be aware of?
- Did your big-picture goal help you stay on track?
- Can you see all your progress in your before and after pictures?
- Onwards and upwards, it's time to tackle the bathroom next.

5

The bathroom

'Your future self will thank you for it.'

We are in the second room on our decluttering journey now. The bathroom is the workhorse of our home. It has to be seriously multi-purpose. A place efficient enough for you to get ready for the day's activities yet calm enough to wind down for a recharge. A place in which to perform the most personal of functions alongside being a sociable playground for children. A sanctuary to shut out the noisy world and a space to invite people into to share a private moment. And these things happen every day, several times a day. Little wonder that a bathroom can quickly become out of control!

Some bathrooms are compact, others are sizable. Some families have one shared bathroom, others have several. Some bathrooms have little to no storage, others have an abundance. But one thing's for sure: bathrooms have a lot of stuff in them and that stuff is varied, plentiful and difficult to navigate. Oh, and did we mention that bathrooms get dirty too? On top of the decluttering and organising, cleaning needs to be non-negotiable as part of any bathroom project.

While a bathroom has its challenges, it's early on in our decluttering journey because there are not that many sentimental things here, which means we can make progress more quickly. Bathrooms are great because there are plenty of quick, easy wins dotted around and we all like a few of those to keep our motivation high, don't we? For example, there will undoubtedly be the odd shampoo bottle that's snuck through the cracks that can be discarded without a second thought. Or a razor that is so grimy it's got rust forming on it. Sound familiar?

Decluttering and organising your bathroom will be super satisfying too on lots of levels. Just straightening up the toiletries and other things we use creates an immediate aesthetic upgrade. Who doesn't want the first room you enter after your eyes pop open to feel calming? And let's face it, most of your bathroom is taken up by a bath or shower, toilet or sink, so storage space is often minimal. Less storage space means less stuff to sort. Well, that's kind of true, but not entirely.

Although it may seem as if the bathroom will be a breeze, there are a couple of trickier bits to factor in. You see, we need to be mindful that the items in a bathroom tend to be on the small side, and the smaller the item, the longer it takes to make visible progress. So, in a bathroom we need to be ready to go granular and get down to the nitty-gritty. Every item needs to be looked at, cleaned and assigned to a sensible, logical home. We must be sure to take the bathroom one step at a time.

It's also in the bathroom where your shopping and acquisition habits are up for scrutiny. It is the room where we keep spares, so the careful management of your **inventory** is paramount. We need to move towards cutting off the clutter at source. We do this by having control of what we have stored and therefore understanding what we need to buy, and this makes a real, sustainable impact on our homes. But don't worry, working through this process will create solid foundations to build upon for the rest of your home. The more light bulbs that go on for you at this stage in your decluttering journey, the easier the process will be further down the line.

JARGON BUSTER

Inventory – the act of gathering similar things together and putting them in order so you know exactly what you have and where it is. This is vital to keep shopping under control and intentional.

So, the bathroom will offer nice easy wins coupled with a few trickier aspects, but, boy oh boy, is it satisfying to get your bathroom (or bathrooms) done. Let's go!

The thinking

Emotional Preparation

So, let's first think about the thoughts and habits we encounter with our bathroom items – the ones that hold us back and keep us stuck. By taking the time to work out which of the following habits and emotions resonate with you, you will be armed with the information that you need in the 'doing' stage on pp. 76–87. Some of the concepts that we will introduce here in this thinking stage will be new to you, but stick with it because in the long term the results will far outweigh any feeling of discomfort you experience right now. Your decluttering muscle is just getting warmed up.

ASPIRATION

The beauty, health and wellness industry is a huge machine. Even at the most basic level, we are faced with an abundance of choice. Way too much choice, if we are being honest. Vitamin C or multivitamin? Lash lengthening or lash building? Moisturising or volumising? There's always something on the shelf or popping up online to pique our interest and challenge our restraint. If you are able to walk past or scroll through that health and beauty section without throwing an extra shampoo in your basket, you're doing well. But why do we buy so much when we are already overrun at home?

The answer is: we are aspirational. Now, we talked about how aspiration holds us back in the kitchen (*see* p. 44), but in the bathroom this is taken to a whole new level. The aspirational trait is at its most prevalent in this room.

The way we look, feel and present ourselves to the world matters to us and we seek out products to help us along the way. Some of us have our trusty favourites that we buy on repeat, but many of us fall foul of shiny object syndrome. If something promises us youth, radiance or improved health, we're all over it and it's just a matter of time before it's part of our new beauty regime.

Dealing with aspirational feelings is taxing, emotional stuff. It's not wrong to want to feel better in yourself but we need to keep things under control. Without self-control, we run the risk of overspending and becoming overwhelmed with products. We need to be confident that the things we buy are both useful and necessary.

Let's face it – we may love something or even need it in our lives, but do we need quite as many variations as we have? That's the question.

OVERBUYING

You've had a stressful time and you just need a mindless activity to decompress. So what do you do? Go shopping, that's what. We've all done it at some point or other. We're human, after all. And the reason shopping feels like a quick, easy fix is all about the dopamine.

When we buy something that excites us, the brain releases endorphins and dopamine. This transitory feeling can lead to compulsive and unintentional shopping, because our minds are tuned to remember how that 'rush' makes us feel. The rush is ultimately more powerful than our willpower.

And once you layer on top of this the marketing machine of the health, beauty and wellness industries, you're definitely in the danger zone. We're surrounded by products and people that promise so much. A designer perfume in a 50 per cent off sale that is just too good to pass by. A coveted beauty brand bag chock-a-block with sample products designed to tempt you when you spend a certain amount. We convince ourselves we would be foolish to let this opportunity go by. And that leads to us buying products that are often just a carbon copy of the ones we already have at home balancing precariously in cupboards unloved and untouched.

Now, getting to grips with intentional shopping and conquering the urge to buy isn't easy and it won't happen overnight. Before you learn the skill of wanting less stuff you need to understand the power of loving space more. Be patient and wait for that decluttering muscle to build, then you'll be able to hit those shops and enjoy the experience, even if you come home with absolutely nothing. For now, begin to recognise this habit and attempt to curb it.

MOVING BEYOND GUILT

If we have succumbed to aspiration or overbuying we will be confronted with our excesses when tackling the bathroom. And what rears its head? Regret, that's what.

Regret, guilt and embarrassment are all intertwined and they are impactful emotions when it comes to the things we have in our homes. Only when we start to gather like with like do we recognise the extent of what we have. We tot up the money we have spent over the years on things that are lying unseen and unused in the bathroom, and then battle to move beyond the guilt.

While guilt is powerful, it's an emotion we need to overcome to allow us to move forwards in our decluttering journeys. But how can we navigate beyond a feeling we may have battled with for years, if not decades? Here's how: we need to get real.

The money was wasted at the time you spent it. No amount of lamenting the loss is going to bring it back. Harsh but true. The guilt is only going to leave you when the item does. If you continue to see that item, it will perpetuate that guilt and stop you in your tracks. Let go of the item, let go of the guilt.

We often feel guilty about the environmental impact of our decluttering, too. Until very recently, there were very few outlets for half-used toiletries, make-up or medication. Thankfully, that's all changing. The very same retailers who are selling beauty and wellness items are offering recycling and incentivisation schemes to encourage you to bring back used products. So, by donating or recycling items and keeping them out of landfill, that's one aspect of guilt we can leave in the past.

But guilt gets even more powerful when we have to navigate not only our own emotions, but those of other people. That's when we are truly tested. We've all been there, haven't we? How can you let go of a hand cream you were given as a gift by a friend or family member even if you know you will never use it? It somehow seems disrespectful, as if we aren't grateful for the thought, care and cost that has gone into the purchase of that gift. But, if we are to succeed in our quest for a clutter-free home, we have to learn to exercise an element of selfishness. We have to put our own needs first. The gift was given to be enjoyed and, if it can't serve that purpose, isn't it better to pass it on to someone who will cherish it?

We harbour a worry that the gift-giver will come into our homes and rifle through our drawers looking for the gift they gave us, but ask yourself whether that has ever happened. It's unlikely. Declutter the item and declutter the guilt associated with it.

EXPIRY CONFUSION

The advisory dates on food are straightforward and easy to understand. The use-by dates on toiletries and make-up on the other hand seem like a dark art. Even though there will undoubtedly be some clever person who can explain the ins and outs of each and every symbol on a product, most of us are a bit clueless! (If you want to know more, a quick search on the internet will help you find out what all those little symbols actually mean, so you're better informed going forwards.) Some of us are organised and will write on a product when it was opened to help us work out when it's expired. Most of us would never do that in a month of Sundays.

So, when it comes to decluttering your bathroom, be ready for the sight and sniff test. Try and make an educated guess about how long something has been open. Whether you think it's necessary to adhere to guidance on how long you should keep things for is your personal choice. If it's been hanging around a while, there's a reason for this. Why has this particular product been overlooked? Do you have others you prefer? Has your style or preference changed perhaps?

Once an item has been buried at the back of a cupboard for a while, and you have absolutely no idea of when that product was opened, you have uncertainty. Uncertainty leads to nervousness, which leads to a 'just in case' mindset. You keep that item just in case it's still good, just in case you've miscalculated how long you've had it, just in case someone else can use it. But that uncertainty also creates a barrier that means you don't instinctively choose it. You'll always favour something you have in your cupboard that you are more certain about and more often than not that is something that's new. The uncertainty you feel means the old one becomes just one more item of clutter.

The expiry date of an item is only one part of the puzzle. Don't let the fact that something is still in date be the excuse to keep it. The real question is why has it been around long enough that it has expired or is about to? Dig deep to challenge those emotions and habits, step out of your comfort zone, remind yourself of your big-picture goal and make a decision on it.

SAVING SAMPLES

You go on a trip, stay in a nice hotel and in the bathroom there's this perfect little row of all kinds of goodies. Two ear buds, a shower cap, shampoo, conditioner, body wash, a shoe shine and, if you're extra lucky, a sewing kit. And then it gets even better. Even though you've only used half of the shampoo, the lovely housekeeping staff give you a fresh new bottle. You have a veritable stash. You paid for it, so why not take it? You come home with your freebies, throw them in with the rest of your toiletries and feel smug that you'll have the perfect thing to take away with you on your next trip and it was free.

Only, there's a problem. On the next trip, you are also staying in a hotel, so you don't need to take any toiletries. In fact, all your trips involve hotels, so you'll never need to take toiletries with you. Even if you did need to take them, they are buried under all your other toiletries, so you have forgotten all about them. Before you know it, the very things you thought were little freebie bonuses have just become lots more clutter.

You have two options here and you need to work out what makes the most sense to you. First, if you can afford to leave those samples behind, learn to say no. It's all part of the 'space over stuff' mindset change we're striving for. But, if saving money makes you tick, your second option is to put a 'Use First' system in place, so you can use the samples immediately at home and will actually make some savings. (We'll explain more on p. 86.)

Once again, your ability to leave samples behind is part of the mindset change you'll begin to undergo on your decluttering journey. These habits have been ingrained and take time to undo. Be patient and be kind to yourself. Your future self will thank you for it.

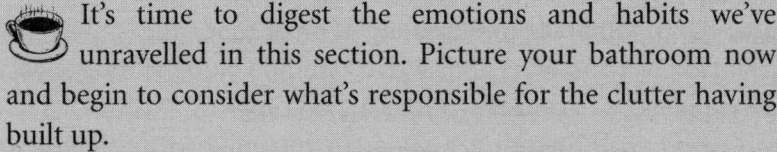

TAKE A MOMENT

It's time to digest the emotions and habits we've unravelled in this section. Picture your bathroom now and begin to consider what's responsible for the clutter having built up.

- Have you succumbed to aspiration? Do you find it impossible to walk past the latest 'must have' product on the beauty aisle?
- Or perhaps you're hooked on the dopamine hit of buying and acquiring more and more?
- Are you wracked with guilt? Do you find it impossible to throw things away because you associate it with wasting money?
- Or is it much simpler? It's just been a while since you've sorted through your things and organised them.

By evaluating which of these emotions resonate with you, we can start to look at emotions first, stuff second. This is the magic formula that will lead to a clutter-free home.

Goal Setting

Let's dive further into our planning by setting some goals. Goals are the key to a successful project but you need to make sure you can differentiate the two types of goals for your bathroom.

BIG-PICTURE GOALS

What kinds of big-picture goals might be your driver in a bathroom? What is your why? Here are some ideas:

- You want to save money by not buying duplicates.
- You want to be able to relax in your bathroom.
- You want to make cleaning easier.
- You want guests to use the loo without you feeling embarrassed.
- You want to save time by finding things easily.

Again, these are suggestions. Your 'why' may be completely different. You may have one of these goals or you may have a combination. The important thing is to understand why a clutter-free bathroom is going to change the game for you. Take a moment now to think about this and even jot it down somewhere if helpful.

Planning Section by Section

Now you have determined your big-picture goal/s, it's time to have a think about how you can break these goals down into an action plan that is much more manageable and can be done step by step.

Use the list below to start decluttering and organising your bathroom category by category:

- Toiletries
- Medication
- Make-up
- Towels
- Toys

Don't forget that you may have bathroom items elsewhere that need to be factored into your declutter. Make-up may be in your bedroom. Medication might be in your kitchen. Towels may be in a linen cupboard. It makes sense to have a full picture of everything in each bathroom-related category as you work through this room. You can decide to declutter things that are elsewhere separately or as part of this project. The important thing is to have a plan, and that plan needs to be managed within the other pulls you have on your time or energy.

Physical Preparation and Logistics

Bathrooms get grimy, so cleaning is going to be a part of the process. We are not just going to tackle the cupboards, drawers and surfaces here. We are going to give the products themselves a wipe too. If something looks clean and fresh it is psychologically far more appealing to use, so it's worth spending a little time on this. Gather together all the cleaning products you are going to use now, so you don't waste time later.

Think about a practical area where you can sort. The floor is just fine if you have space, if it's clean and makes sense to you physically. Temporary boxes can also be useful for sorting things like medication and make-up, so if you have them, now's the time to grab them. And obviously you'll need a bin bag or two for any rubbish.

Think about your exit plan. Where are the things you declutter going to go? Get your recycling bags at the ready and prepare to empty and rinse bottles and jars. It's unlikely that there's going to be too much in your bathroom that belongs elsewhere in your house, but you never know, so grab a box or bag for things that need to be rehomed to the rooms they belong in.

How long it will take to declutter your bathroom varies but it is certainly possible to do most bathrooms in a few hours. Because we are likely to need the bathroom to be functional again today, we may need to put more time into this room in one go than in other rooms in our homes.

If you have multiple bathrooms you need to ask yourself if you can do one bathroom at a time or if you have time to do them all together.

And now it's photo time. Take a 'before' picture or video of your whole bathroom and inside your cupboards, drawers and containers. It's important to have that visual record so you can see later how far you've come.

The doing

How and Where to Get Started

It's not tricky to know where to start in a bathroom. Most of us only have one or two areas in which to store items, so there aren't many choices.

That said, everyone's volumes, storage and drivers are different. If you have a make-up collection that would rival Bobbi Brown's then that category is going to take time. If you have one lipstick, a blusher and a mascara or no make-up in sight, you can tick this category off super quick.

The ideal way to get started in your bathroom is to sort items out one category at a time, but if everything is jumbled together, you are going to need to bite the bullet and spend time categorising and evaluating concurrently.

A bathroom can be overwhelming, not just because of the stuff but because of the cleaning involved too, so it's so important to recognise cleaning is an integral part of the process and factor that in, however cumbersome.

So, grab some cleaning products and start your decluttering.

Decluttering Category by Category

EASY WINS

Before we tackle the tougher emotions we've mentioned, the good news is that there are a lot of things in a bathroom that should be easy to let go of because they are past their best. Brace yourself for some quick-fire, no-brainer decisions, such as:

- Toiletries that are congealed or separated. No-brainer.
- Make-up that looks grimy or clumpy. No-brainer.
- Medication that's expired. No-brainer.
- Rusty old razors or nail files. No-brainer.
- Bristle-challenged toothbrushes or capless toothpaste tubes. No-brainer.
- Chargers and electric toothbrushes you no longer use. No-brainer.

- The tiny remnants of a bar of soap stuck to your soap dish. No-brainer.
- Sun cream that's more than a season old. No-brainer.
- Bath toys full of mould. No-brainer.
- Empty toilet roll holders. Why oh why are they still hanging around? No-brainer.

You get the drift…

There are a lot of random things that get buried among other stuff in a bathroom that present you with what should be an easy decision.

However, just a little caveat here: sometimes even no-brainer decisions can take serious energy to acknowledge. If this is you then don't worry. Hopefully just knowing that these suggestions should be easy wins will help reframe your thinking. Slowly but surely you will become more confident and learn to be able to let things go.

Dig deeper

In order to really drill down on decluttering the bathroom we need to look at the volume of items we have. Where are our duplicates? Which are our favourites? In order to take our decision-making to the next level, we need to gather like with like and evaluate. Gathering all of a certain type of item together will allow us to confront ourselves with the reality of what we have kept. Is the number of a particular type of item we have excessive, or does it make sense given the circumstances of our lives? Arming ourselves with this knowledge and reality allows us to challenge our norm and make sensible decisions.

Categorisation is *everything* when it comes to the things in your bathroom. Depending on the storage you have or will use in the long term you may have to amalgamate some of your things when you store them but, for now, declutter your bathroom items using these categories. You may have some of them, you may have all of them, but by tackling one category at a time if possible, you will feel a greater sense of control and accomplishment.

HAIR PRODUCTS

Gather together both the items you use in the shower and the stuff you use for styling. Depending on the style of your hair, this can mount up. Bring them all into one place: the stuff from the shower caddy, the items in your cupboard, the ones from your weekly shop you've not put away yet, the rogue ones you got as part of a gift set. They all need to be in one place so you can make decisions. Do you have ones that you will always favour over others?

MANICURE AND PEDICURE PRODUCTS

Some people love a home manicure or pedicure, so if that's you, gather together those creams, scrubs and rubs, and nail polish too. Be honest about your routines. How often will you use the things you are storing and do they justify the space they are taking up?

DENTAL PRODUCTS

Teeth paraphernalia adds up and we need to keep it hygienic and store it together. Are you a simple soul with just a toothbrush and toothpaste or do you have floss, interdental brushes, whitening kit and electric toothbrush chargers? Are the things we are keeping hygienic enough to still be in use?

SHAVING EQUIPMENT AND HAIR REMOVAL

Whether it's manual or electric, face or body, it needs a home and we need to keep those sharp blades away from vulnerable fingers. Is that hair removal stuff still safe? Have we changed the way we remove hair now?

BODY CARE

Creams, serums, bath oils, shower gels, exfoliators and lots more besides. This category involves bigger pots too, which creates the additional challenge of fitting them into the space. Do we have favourites we are replacing when they run out while we still have others that are perfectly functional, but lower down the list of preferences?

FACE CARE

If you're a make-up and skincare fan and sub-categorisation here makes sense, now's the time to work out what categories of items you use every day to put your best face forwards to the world. Are there items that didn't suit your skin? Are there items you have had for years but never reach for?

SANITARY PRODUCTS

These can be bulky and you need reserves, so put them in a category of their own. You may choose to store them out of the bathroom but do factor them into this project. Do the volumes you have reflect your needs or do you have reserves that are excessive?

DEODORANT

You've probably only got one or two, but if you have multiple people using one bathroom the numbers can add up. Did you buy a body spray you bought by mistake with no anti-perspirant qualities that you are keeping as a back-up?

SUN CARE

This may or may not be kept in your bathroom, but it's good to have a feel for how many you have and keep them all together so you're not exposed if the sun unexpectedly pops out. Do you have sun cream that's over a season old? Do you have a very low or very high factor that you only used once?

WASH BAGS

We need to make an assessment about just how many wash bags and make-up bags we have because we so often get them as freebies. To help us evaluate, we need to gather them all in one place and confront ourselves with the numbers. How often do you use them? Do you have a favourite size? Have you got ones you've not used in years?

BATH TOYS

If you have young kids at home, you're going to need to find a sensible solution for bath toys, so gather them in one place and make some decisions. Are they age appropriate? Are your kids choosing them on a regular basis? Are you nervous about what germs may be inside?

MEDICATION AND FIRST AID

It's vital to have a handle on medication and first aid because the last thing we need is to be hunting high and low when we are not feeling in the best shape. Medication is tough because it feels so expensive and wasteful to let something go that's still in date, but we need to be realistic. Did you buy something for an ailment that's cleared up? Has your doctor switched you to a new prescription? Be honest about your medication supplies; identify what you use frequently and what you would need in an emergency.

FREE SAMPLES

Gather any free samples together so you can create a system to use them up and save yourself some money. Look at use-by dates. Will you adhere to a 'Use First' system? Do you have more than you could ever use? Could this be the first step towards weaning yourself off freebie gathering?

TOWELS

With towels, once you have decluttered the tatty or greying ones, look at the number you have and make an assessment on whether you have too many. Be honest with yourself. The fewer towels you have, the easier they are to manage. Are you keeping an excess of towels because your laundry isn't under control and you fear you will run out?

BITS AND BOBS

There are a few other categories not to miss: bathrobes, flannels and sponges, beauty and skincare tools and gadgets, and cleaning products. All of these things are found and used in a bathroom, so if they are in yours, gather them together so you can check you have the right amount and can allocate them to a sensible storage place.

Don't forget to repatriate things that have found their way out of the bathroom. Toiletries from your gym bag, that lipstick from your work bag, the sun lotion from the beach bag. Gather, gather, gather so again you have a full picture of how many of everything you have and whether or not they are worthy of the space they will command in your bathroom.

Storage Solutions

The likelihood is that you already have storage in your bathroom, but now's the time for you to have a think about whether it is really working for you. Are you happy with what you have or do you need to make some changes? It doesn't matter if you have a small bathroom, a large bathroom, an en-suite bathroom or a bathroom you share with four or five people – getting the storage right is absolutely critical. Using the right storage allows your items to be accessible and visible, and it also ensures that cleaning and tidying your bathroom is a breeze.

We are huge advocates of not buying new storage solutions until you have a full picture of what it is you need going forwards and indeed whether any changes are needed at all. But by now you have decluttered no-brainers, sorted items into categories, looked at the volumes you have and dug deeper again. You have managed to get to a stage where you are happy with the decisions you have made and the things you are keeping, so it's time to think about storage.

Look at each item you are keeping to determine how tall it is, how wide it is, what shape it is and how many you have of it in each category. This will allow you to evaluate what kind of storage is going to be helpful when it comes to organising your bathroom. Be aware of what you use daily and what you use less frequently, and remember to be realistic about the space you have.

If you are sourcing new storage solutions then you may have a timing issue. For example, you may not be able to go to the shops right away or it may be a few days until your online delivery arrives. Therefore, at this point feel free to use temporary storage boxes, such as storage you already have, shoe boxes or cardboard boxes from around the home. Then you'll be able to fine-tune, tweak and swap things over when your new storage arrives.

There are lots of different options when it comes to bathroom storage. It can be easy to put problems you have with organising this room down to the fact that your bathroom just won't accommodate some of the more versatile and sizable storage that's available. But your home is your home, so you need to make the most of what you have, find clever solutions and be mindful of the pitfalls. Let's talk through some important things to consider when thinking about how to store your bathroom items.

CONTAINERISATION

The secret weapon of bathroom organisation is containerisation. All those little categories you created earlier need to be stored together in the right-size containers for each. The space you are working with is going to dictate what you can use. Grab your tape measure and start to do some calculations. How many containers can you fit side by side in your cupboard or drawer? How deep is your space? You need to find a box that is not so tall that you are compromising visibility and accessibility, but tall enough that you are not wasting space above. Go for straight not slanted sides, and opt for square and rectangular rather than round and oval (don't let those valuable inches slip away unused). Choose material that is easy to clean and not susceptible to damp or water. Will the box accommodate a label? Do you need it to have a handle? Lids off are preferable and stackable is ideal if you have tall shelves or large volumes of stuff. It's worth investing the time to find the right container as it can be an absolute game-changer to the efficiency and aesthetic of your bathroom. Who knew choosing a box could be so complex?

CUPBOARDS AND CABINETS

Bathroom cabinets come in all different shapes and sizes. They are perfect for being easily accessible and enabling you to see what you need, as they are at eye level. If you have a mirror over your sink, investigate whether you can incorporate a cabinet behind it. A mirror without a cabinet is a wasted opportunity if you are tight on space. Choose a cabinet that maximises the space – if you can go deeper, do it. You can never have enough storage in a bathroom.

At first glance, a sink unit with drawers underneath looks like a fantastic solution, but it's not as good as it seems. A lot of the space is taken up by pipework so your storage space can be compromised. In a showroom, there's not a pipe in sight, but once you install it, the space you thought you'd have rapidly disappears because of those pesky pipes. Having said that, they are a great solution for accessibility because they are located right where you stand at the sink and, because you are looking straight down into them, visibility is good too. You can use these drawers for products you use every day, but the chances are you will still need extra storage somewhere else as it's rarely enough.

Some bathrooms have a nice big cupboard, which is brilliant if you have large volumes of items to store. Solid shelves are perfect but if they are slatted, you might need to change them over. Think about adding extra shelves too if they are very far apart, as this will double your available space.

If you have a spare wall anywhere, a full-height bathroom cupboard is a dream solution. The taller you can go with your bathroom storage the better. Even if you don't feel you need extra space it will allow you to categorise and containerise more effectively.

THINKING OUTSIDE THE BOX

Sometimes you have no storage options at all in the bathroom and every bit of available space is taken up by baths, showers, windows, radiators and doors. This is when you need to be inventive, but don't despair! There are many ways to get creative in the bathroom, so let's talk through some of these now.

If you have a decent depth of windowsill, this is the perfect place to house boxes.

If your bathroom is used for kids' play, you are going to need a spot for bath toys. You can use a mesh bag that hooks over the taps or attaches to the bath with suction pads. A plastic box is also an option but make sure the box has drainage as bath toys that sit in water can quickly become mouldy. The main thing is not to leave them in the bath or on the floor. If there's one thing that is going to upset the tranquillity in your bathroom it's toys, so try and source a clever solution.

If you can use the back of your door, that's an option too. You can buy overdoor hanging with tiered mesh or plastic pockets and these can work well if you are tight on space elsewhere. Small beauty products are ideal in this kind of storage as long as you ensure the compartments are see-through for greater visibility.

If you don't need the back of your bathroom door to store your products, you could use it for bathrobes, dressing gowns or towels. Hooks are fantastic but choose ones that screw in rather than stick on (bathrobes and towels are heavy and adhesive hooks just can't hold the weight). If you have space for one hook per person, you can also assign everyone their own dedicated towel space.

A shelf above or next to your sink can be useful if you need or want the things you use most frequently out on display. But don't let the shelf become overcrowded. Tumblers for toothpaste and toothbrushes can easily topple so it's always a great idea to have a toothbrush holder screwed into the wall if you can.

A shower caddy is handy to keep your shower gel, shampoo and conditioner close by. The multi-tiered versions are the most useful if it is a family bathroom. Look at rust-free options as it's worth investing in one that will last, particularly if you are drilling into the wall to fix it in place.

If you have the option to get something created bespoke, make sure you do your declutter first and work out exactly what height and depth it needs to be to maximise storage. You don't want to lose any space anywhere. If shelves can be adjustable, that's even better.

There are so many inventive options available for both larger spaces and ones where space is at a premium. Now you know what you are working with from a volume and space perspective, it's time to analyse whether what you have is sufficient, then do your research and find a storage solution that's going to work for you. Don't forget, if you need to reinstate your bathroom so it can be used later today, use temporary storage until your replacements arrive.

Organisation and Categorisation

So we've decluttered what we don't need, made some decisions about storage and maybe even treated ourselves to something new. Now it's time to put things where they need to be. This is the nice part, when you make things look neat, tidy and organised. And it might take a few goes to get it right, so be patient. Don't be scared to make changes if a system hasn't worked for you before. Try something different. The worst thing that can happen is that you need to change it in a week or two. So, let's start putting the puzzle pieces together.

If you still have things in your bathroom you no longer need, now's the time to get them out of the bathroom, ready for recycling or donation. If items need to be moved to other rooms, do that too so you have clear space in which to lay out your containers.

As you start to work through your categorised items, first give them a wipe so they look their best. Start thinking about whether you have space for each category to have its own container or whether you need to amalgamate some. When deciding where to put your containers, think about visibility and accessibility. Have the things you are using every day close at hand and the infrequent-use items a little further from reach. If you need to combine a few categories, tap into logic. Which of the categories make sense together? You may need to think about size too. So, for example, you may place all the tall bottles together. Think about the system you have used in the past and where it fell short. Accessibility, visibility and logic should be your focus. You have thought about this in the kitchen, and it's time to revisit it now in your bathroom.

If you have a small bathroom with limited storage you may need to only keep your essential products to hand and store the rest elsewhere. It could be a drawer in the bedroom, a box in the linen cupboard or a cupboard in your storage room.

Although we are huge advocates of donating surplus items, many of the things in the bathroom are consumable and therefore can and will be used at some point. They have added to our clutter simply because we have lost track when shopping and have too many for our current needs. As long as they have adequate shelf life they too can be moved to an overflow area. This may be in a bedroom cupboard, a hallway or landing cupboard, or a utility room. It's important that it is easy to access and you have a clear idea of what is there. That way, it will stay front of mind and facilitate 'shopping from home'. Being able to shop from home and know that you are using up your excess is hugely satisfying. And once that overflow area is depleted, you won't need it any more and that's another empty cupboard or drawer. Win–win!

Be mindful not to bulk-buy if you are short on space. Unless an item is very difficult to buy or you get a very good deal on it, we would suggest only having one extra. If an item is difficult to get hold of, you might want to get at most a couple of spares, but be aware you will be compromising on your space. The goal should be for you to be able to store everything in the room you use it in, so ideally your overflow area will be just a temporary solution.

Create a prominent 'Use First' container. Gather together sample sizes from hotels along with half-empty bottles of shampoo, conditioner and body wash. Have a non-negotiable rule to use the smallest items first so you can make an impact on excess quickly. Reduce the number of containers in your bathroom and save yourself some precious money. What's not to love?

By now your cupboards will be clean and your items will be containerised. You may need to do a bit of tweaking here and there;

it's unusual to get everything in the right place immediately. You may need to compromise a little to make your system fit where you'd like it to.

The Finishing Touches

Do a final thorough clean of the rest of your bathroom. Now your surfaces are clear and your items are in place, it will take much less time than before. That finishing touch will make all the difference and encourage you to keep your bathroom looking at its best.

Last but not least, labelling containers can also help you find items you need. You can opt to keep a label simple and functional or go all out for the look. There are some beautiful bespoke solutions out there or you can use a label maker or a sticker.

And we're almost done! Take the things you are donating or recycling to their final destination. Charity shops, homeless shelters, beauty stores, giveaway groups, raffles and tombolas are all possibilities for you to pass your things on. Depending on where you live, you may be able to return medication to a pharmacy for safe disposal.

The enjoyment that comes when you have decluttered and organised your bathroom is one you will experience over and over because you use it every day. You will start your day with a brighter outlook and end your day with a calmer feeling. No need to wade through half-empty shampoo bottles on your shower floor. All your daily skincare can sit neatly side by side and is easy to access.

Take an 'after' photo so you have a record of what you've achieved. If you are struggling to remember how far you've come, scroll back to your 'before' pictures and compare them with what you are looking at now. Can you see that your decision-making is getting easier and your ability to evaluate your organisation is getting more intuitive? If so, that's your decluttering muscle getting nicely warmed up!

Well done, that's another tough room ticked off your list.

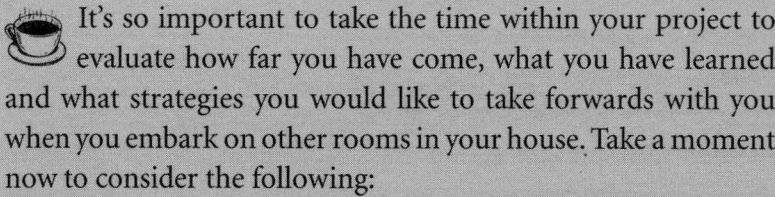

TAKE A MOMENT

It's so important to take the time within your project to evaluate how far you have come, what you have learned and what strategies you would like to take forwards with you when you embark on other rooms in your house. Take a moment now to consider the following:

- How important was it for you to declutter and organise your bathroom?
- Have you worked out the habits and emotions that have led you to keeping an excess of things in your bathroom?
- Have you learnt anything from working on your bathroom that will help you build your decluttering muscle?

6

The bedroom

'Seek out possibility rather than impossibility.'

If you sit back and reflect on why you feel overwhelmed by your clutter, you can bet your bottom dollar that a large part of it stems from clothes. The clothes packed to the rafters in your wardrobe, the **floordrobe** that's growing day after day, that pile of laundry that's winking at you as you go about your daily business. Let's face it, we all have clothes. We all need clothes. Clothes are what make us ready to face the day ahead. Clothes are what people notice when they meet us. Clothes are what make us safe, warm, glamorous, comfortable or unique. They have a purpose. One thing that everyone on the planet has in common is clothes. They are non-negotiable in our lives. But the question really is – how do we make sure we have the right amount in the right place at the right time?

JARGON BUSTER

Floordrobe – a pile of clothing that has not found its way back into the wardrobe, either due to procrastination or an overfull space.

When we ask people what rooms bother them most, trust us, the bedroom is always high on the list. Yet we neglect it all the time. Why?

Because we can. We neglect this room because no one else has reason to go in there. The bedroom isn't the first place that springs to mind when you want to have a cup of tea with your best friend. It's a private space so we choose to ignore it and prioritise the communal areas of our homes – the ones that others see and may judge.

Being judged is a huge driver when it comes to how we feel about clutter and our decluttering journey. If you have struggled with stuff for most or some of your life, you will undoubtedly have been subject to criticism – from a partner fed up with the chaos, from a parent exhausted by an untidy bedroom, from a child who is reluctant to have their friends over, from a friend who desperately wants to help you declutter and fix the problem, from a tradesman who can't easily get to the boiler he's trying to fix or from a nosy neighbour who stares into your hallway when they deliver a parcel to you. These judgements hurt and we digest each and every one directed our way.

When deciding which room needs attention first, we therefore choose communal areas, areas other people visit, areas that, if left untouched, might mean that judgement will come our way. We prioritise other people's experiences above our own, but should we?

No. We deserve a bedroom that is calm and distraction-free. Sleeping, relaxing, reading, making love – all these things are best done distraction-free. The bedroom should be a sanctuary and if it's rammed with piles of clothes, books, toiletries, keepsakes, laptops and shoes then it's hard to not be distracted by the stuff of life.

So, it's time to make that happen.

But, first, the reality check – it's not going to be easy. A bedroom involves some testing and emotional decisions, and we need to be ready for them. The kitchen and bathroom involved delving into easier emotions, but the bedroom will take things up a notch. But you're ready for this now. You've been warming up your decluttering muscle in the first two rooms and now we're ready to test it further.

We're going to focus first and foremost on clothes because they typically make up a huge part of the challenge when it comes to the bedroom. People who have a lot of clutter often have high volumes of clothes, so it's going to take some time, but it will be so worth it. Are you in?

So, set your goals, do your preparation and get ready for a transformation. Let's dive into those emotions and habits first and then come up with a practical plan to declutter and organise your bedroom.

The thinking

Emotional Preparation

Now, decluttering certain things in your bedroom can actually be quite simple. Those socks with holes in and that jewellery that's out of fashion don't take any emotional energy to decide upon, so we can make serious progress just with some basic questions: Do I need it?, Do I use it? and Do I love it? These questions are a great starting place but they are not going to cut the mustard when we get stuck.

You see, it won't be long once you start a clothing declutter before doubts begin to creep in. You're looking at an item and confusion is building. I don't need it today, but I might one day. I don't use it today, but I'd love to one day. I do love it but then I love everything every day. Do you see where we're going with this…? Decluttering is never as simple as the magazines and YouTube videos would have us believe. If it were, you wouldn't have bought this book.

So, let's talk about the thoughts that keep us stuck and how to remedy that when it comes to clothing.

WEIGHT WORRIES

First up, something many of us are familiar with: worrying about weight. If you are someone whose weight never changes, then we applaud your focus and willpower and envy your metabolism. But for everyone else the things we are talking about here may resonate with you.

Our weight is likely to change regularly throughout our lives. Whether that's an unwanted weight loss or gain, both bring with them a struggle, sometimes lifelong. This can lead to continual soul-searching. How long will you be this weight? Do you have the tools to change it? Do you have the willpower and determination to carry a transformation through? Where does your stuff fit into this weight change? Should you let go of clothes that are too big or small even though there's a chance you'll get back into them one day. That would be a waste, right?

This is where you need to dig deep into realism. How realistic is it that you can lose or gain those 10 or 20 pounds that you've been struggling with? Is a wardrobe full of clothes you can't wear helping with your self-esteem?

If you have been struggling for years and are three sizes up from the clothes hanging in your wardrobe, then perhaps it's time to let that idea go and move forwards with decluttering the things that don't fit. But only you know your life, your historic patterns of behaviour and what the likelihood of success is going to be. It's you and only you who can be realistic about this. You have the final say.

Why is it so important to let go of things that don't fit? Where's the harm in living in hope for that change? Well, because each time you open that wardrobe door you are confronted with impossibility rather than possibility, negative feelings rather than positive ones, and that's not a great way to start your day. Wouldn't it be nice to open your wardrobe door and see only things in it that fit? Only clothing that you can actually wear here and now. Honestly, making this change will allow you to start your day or your evening in a more positive frame of mind. Seeing possibility rather than impossibility in your wardrobe is a powerful shift.

GATHERING GO-TOS

What's a go-to item? It might be a little black dress, a comfy pair of joggers, pyjamas, black trousers, a fleece top, a certain style of bra – it doesn't matter what it is – the point is that when you find something that works, that never lets you down, you crave more, so you buy more.

There are so many reasons why we have go-to items. They feel good on you, you like the way they hang, they're flattering, comfy, comforting, forgiving, good quality or good value for money. We each have our own reason for our go-to item and it's different for everyone. For example:

- It's that sweater you buy in pink, blue, green, navy, beige and purple (even though you don't really love purple) because it doesn't let you down.
- It's that pair of pyjamas you just can't walk past because you love the cosiness PJs bring when you're ready to binge that boxset.
- It's that little black dress that everyone compliments (and who doesn't love a compliment?).
- It's that 17th pair of black jeans because you can never have enough black jeans, right?

You get the gist.

So, what's the problem? Isn't it a good thing to have items that work well for us? Yes and no. The problem is you can have too many. If we have 10 versions of our favourite jumper, when we are getting ready to go out we will instinctively choose maybe our first, second or third favourite, but we are unlikely ever to get to number six or seven, so they sit in our wardrobes unworn and unloved, taking up space.

By recognising this subconscious need to crave more and more of the same go-to item, we can cut down on volumes and steer ourselves towards a clutter-free home.

BREAK THROUGH BARRIERS

Who knew clothing would have barriers associated with it? Yes, there are barriers by the bucketload when it comes to clothes and shoes and, once again, they are typically subconscious. So, let's explore them.

There is a regularly quoted concept that we wear 20 per cent of our clothes 80 per cent of the time. And our experiences with most clients would support that. But why? What is it about the other 80 per cent of clothes that means we pass them by each time? Now, it will most certainly be for the reasons we have already mentioned, but also often there's something that just doesn't feel right and we can't quite put our finger on what it is.

In simple terms it might be that a top is too short or a pair of trousers is too tight, but what if we dig a little deeper? It might be something about how our bodies feel in certain clothes, something more subconscious that stops us from wearing something. For example, it could be:

- a top that gapes when we are sitting down;
- a skirt that shows a part of our legs we aren't proud of;
- a bra that digs in and leaves a mark;
- a jumper that itches.

When we last wore that item it just didn't work well, but we like it so much that we want to try again. But we bypass it when we are choosing our clothes for the day, and it sits firmly in the 80 per cent unworn clothes category.

Only by spending time evaluating an item can we work out whether it has a barrier attached to it that is stopping us from making a proactive choice to wear it. And when decluttering we need to dig deep to understand what those barriers might be.

CHALLENGING CHANGE

Clothing is an outward representation of how we are feeling. And throughout our lives we are going to have different types of clothing that represent different times of our lives. As transitions come our way, they often bring with them a shift in wardrobe choices.

So, what types of life transitions are we talking about and how might they affect our wardrobe? Examples include:

- a career change that means what worked in one workplace doesn't in another;
- having a baby, which means comfort and practicality take precedence;
- a house move to an area where you may need warmer or cooler clothes;
- a retirement, meaning you no longer need to use your 'corporate' wardrobe;
- ill health that stops you wearing certain clothes or shoes.

Some of these transitions are welcome, enriching and straightforward, but some are not. Many of these periods represent times when we were at our most fulfilled and happy. Saying goodbye to those parts of our lives can be tough. Adding to that loss by decluttering the clothes you wore during this period can make things even harder.

We need to acknowledge, therefore, that even though accepting transitions readily seems like a no-brainer, we might just not be there yet. A decluttering journey is not a one-and-done project. It is a process that takes time. The most important part of this process is that you feel in control of the decisions you are making right here, right now. And, if necessary, and when you're ready, you can do a further round.

GIVING UP GUILT

Guilt plays a big part in the types of clutter we have in our bedrooms for two main reasons: the money we spent on it or the person who gave it to us. This is simple to understand but a hard thing to work through because guilt is such a strong emotion. It holds us to ransom.

Let's talk about money first. Imagine the scene – we see a beautiful pair of shoes; we try them on and they're perfect. The price tag means they are an extravagant purchase, but it's going to be so worth it. We go on our first outing with our beautiful new shoes on, and we start to struggle an hour into the evening. We get a horrendous blister, go home, put them back on the shelf. We give them a second chance a few weeks later but it's the same outcome. Blistered feet and one very expensive pair of shoes winking at us from the bottom of the wardrobe each time we walk past.

But do we declutter them? Of course we don't, because guilt kicks in. We try to convince ourselves that maybe our feet will change and we won't get a blister next time. Maybe we will get them stretched – all manner of things that we work through in our minds because we feel guilty about the amount they cost and our inability to get our money's worth. And every time we see that pair of shoes our guilt is perpetuated.

Second, we have the guilt that comes from unwanted gifts. That scarf from a friend, which we couldn't bear the moment we saw it, or that bag of hand-me-downs from our sister-in-law we know we'll never use. We feel obligated to keep them because of the guilt related to them. We know they have no place in our lives, but we keep hold of them out of a sense of duty to the person who gave them to us.

Flicking the switch from a feeling of guilt to acceptance is tough – the gift-giver may have been a child, a partner, a parent or a best friend. How can we be so disrespectful as to declutter something that has a kind thought behind it? The reason this is so hard is because it crosses a line into other people's emotions and not just our own. The reality is very few people come to your house demanding to see a gift they gave you two years ago and rifle through your drawers to find it. But we still think they will. Guilt can have a stranglehold on us, can't it?

Selling Stuff

So, we've processed the fact that we feel guilty about things in our homes that we spent money on in the past, and while we recognise that trait, we just can't help ourselves but try to alleviate that guilt. How do we think we can do that? By selling our stuff. Or should I say, by putting stuff into a pile, a bag, a loft or a garage with the intention to sell it? Because the selling for most of us so rarely happens.

We can't even tell you how many bags of 'stuff for eBay' we've seen in people's homes (and minds) that stops them from achieving their decluttering goals. In fact, by putting items into a corner to sell we are not actually decluttering at all, we are **churning** items around our homes and giving ourselves even more jobs to do.

JARGON BUSTER

Churning – the act of moving items earmarked for decluttering but keeping them in a pile, either delaying a decision or while waiting to sell or donate, thereby not decluttering them at all.

But how do you fix this? First and foremost, you need to have clarity around your goal. Is the goal to make money or to declutter? These are two very different things and it's vitally important to work out which is the priority. One of the big problems with selling things, particularly clothes, is that we have an elevated idea of what something is worth. When it sells for peanuts, we are disappointed. This detracts from all the hard work we have done decluttering. So, it presents a lose–lose situation.

If, on the other hand, we accept that the money was spent in good faith at the time of purchase, allow ourselves to buy into the feel-good emotion that donation brings, and save ourselves time, energy and hassle, we can speed ahead with our decluttering and move closer to our goals.

Only you know whether selling is a good idea for you. As long as you have a plan and can execute on it quickly and efficiently, selling items can most certainly add even more value to a positive process. But in our experience, more often than not, it doesn't.

To sell or not to sell: that is the question. You know what we think. Now it's over to you to dig into the reality of your own past behaviours.

Sorting Out Sentimental

Now, you will undoubtedly have things in your wardrobe that are truly sentimental – the outfit you wore when you got engaged, the T-shirt from a gig by your favourite band, or a wedding outfit. At this stage the most important thing is to recognise that these things are sentimental and need to be left until much later in your decluttering journey. As already outlined, we need to build up your decluttering muscle more before we attempt this. Working through your clothes in this chapter will form a key part of your learning. So put your sentimental items aside for now and we'll revisit them in Chapter 12.

TAKE A MOMENT

As we work our way through our homes room by room, we will come across new emotions we haven't encountered before. The bedroom is no exception. It's time to look at your things to determine which ones are holding you back from having a functional wardrobe space. At this point, let's reflect on the following:

- Are you clinging on to too many clothes in the hope you'll fit back into them one day?
- Have you found a clothing item that never lets you down that has become your go-to?
- Are you able to identify little niggly things about a garment that stop you choosing it?
- Are you struggling to move on past a key period of your life and hanging on to the clothes relating to it?
- Have you made mistake purchases in the past that trouble you so much you keep the item out of guilt?
- Do you then try and fix that guilty feeling by making plans to sell things but that just never happens?

Goal Setting

Setting a big-picture goal for your bedroom is so important. You'll notice that most of the emotions we've mentioned are related to just clothes, and that's for good reason. You see, ideally a bedroom should contain clothes, shoes, bags, accessories, a few bits and bobs in your bedside table to see you through your sleep time and not much else. What we should be aiming for is a calming space, and if we have lots of other types of random items in the bedroom then they are going to detract from the primary purpose in this room.

Now, we are not foolish enough to think that every home is that simple. We all need to make compromises to factor in the space we have to live with but, if you can, let your goals for your bedroom reflect a determined shift towards a more restful environment overall.

BIG-PICTURE GOALS

What kinds of big-picture goals might relate to a bedroom and in particular clothing? Perhaps you'd like to:

- Cut down on the decision-making required before work in relation to your clothes.
- Ensure everything in your wardrobe is suitable for your current lifestyle and values.
- Stop wasting money on overbuying clothing because you're not sure what you have.
- Ensure all your clothes are contained in *your* bedroom, so that having guests to stay in your spare bedroom doesn't become troublesome.
- Eradicate floordrobes, chairdrobes, and laundry or ironing piles from your bedroom.

When you've decided on your big-picture goal, take a few minutes to note it down so you can refer back to it to motivate you in the future. Then it's time to decide how to break this down. There's just a little more pre-planning to do and then we'll be ready to get cracking.

Planning Section by Section

You need to split down your clothing section by section otherwise it becomes an overwhelming task. Try to work one wardrobe section or one drawer at a time.

This would be our ideal way to break down your bedroom into manageable sections:

- Hanging clothes one wardrobe section at a time
- Folded clothes one drawer at a time
- Shoes
- Accessories
- Bedside table drawers
- Bedside table surfaces
- Under the bed
- Top of the wardrobe
- Jewellery

If you have make-up, toiletries or medication in your bedroom, refer back to Chapter 5. If you have sentimental items in your bedroom, these need to wait until later in your decluttering journey, so put them aside for now.

Physical Preparation and Logistics

Planning is key in each and every room of your home. In the bedroom we need to be ready for what's coming. You'll be surprised by just how many items of clothing you have. Every one of these items needs a decision and so it's going to take some time to work through them.

It's also helpful to have a full overview of what you have, so, if practical, make sure your washing and ironing is up to date before you do your decluttering session. Inevitably, there are going to be clothes that need a wash, so be sure to have a laundry basket close at hand to throw things into as you find them.

Bin bags in different colours will help you feel in control of the process. For example, you can assign a different-coloured bin bag for things for your friend, things to be mended and things to donate to charity. This will ensure you have a clear picture of what goes where at the end of your session.

Make your bed so you have a flat surface to work on once you start to take things out of your wardrobe or find another large, flat area that will work. Open the window, as clothes can be dusty and musty and it's nice to have fresh air. Grab the vacuum cleaner and some cloths so you can clean as you go, too. Cleaning your space adds to the feeling of satisfaction at the end.

We aren't advocates of buying storage too early in the process but there's always an exception that proves the rule and a coat hanger is just that. A thin velvet hanger can be a game-changer in a wardrobe. They are lightweight, space-saving, aesthetically uniform and readily available to buy. If your wardrobe is currently a mishmash of all kinds of hangers you may want to swap them over to a new version.

Although it's important to make clear that upgrading your hangers is absolutely not vital and will not change your decluttering outcome, if you would like to go that step further and change your hangers, then before you begin is the time to make your purchases. Do a quick tot up of how many items you have in your wardrobe and order enough hangers to cover that. (You'll be surprised at the numbers – it can run to hundreds!) Ensure you have the option to return any unused hangers so that, if your decluttering goes well, you are not left with too many spares.

And finally, take those 'before' photos. They will serve as a key reminder of just how much progress you are making.

The doing

How and Where to Get Started

When it comes to a bedroom it pays to get started in an area where you are going to make tangible progress and see big wins, so the best place is the hanging section of your clothing.

Rule number one is don't take all items out of all wardrobes at once. It's too overwhelming and can damage your clothes if they are all piled up and threatening to topple. Work on one wardrobe section at a time. Small, manageable chunks are the aim here.

But do take items out of your wardrobe. Don't try and declutter them by trying to force clothes apart on the rail inside your wardrobe and having only a cursory glance. No swishing allowed here! They need to come out. And there's a psychological reason for this: once something has been taken out of a wardrobe you need to make a proactive decision to put it back in. If it's sitting in the same place it always has, we don't see it with a fresh pair of eyes, and it's important to see something in a different light to the way that we have been seeing it for years on a hanging rail. And of course, taking items out means you can clean the space unhindered.

If you identify things to get rid of as you are taking them out of your wardrobe they can be decluttered straight away. It may be useful to do a pre-sort at this stage into broad categories, too, so you have a better handle on the quantity of each type of item you have. Pre-sorting just means gathering like with like as you take things out of your wardrobe. Often, you will already have established some categorisation with your clothes in your wardrobe, although it may have gone a little awry over time.

Move through the sections in your bedroom one at a time so you can keep the process controlled, and finish or take a break when you start to tire.

Leave the smaller areas till last as they involve fiddly items. Clearing out your bedside table or working through your jewellery can be so satisfying but it takes a lot of time, so build up to that later in the bedroom process (but be sure not to overlook these areas completely!).

Decluttering Questions

We've now done the thinking. We've evaluated our own past and current behaviours, so by now we are armed with self-awareness about some of the reasons we have been holding on to things that don't serve us well in our current lives. We know how we're going to approach the bedroom. So, it's time to step out of our comfort zone and start making progress. Are you ready to start flexing that decluttering muscle?

When we are going through the process of decluttering thoroughly, we need to invest ample time. Try on the clothes, look in the mirror, ask for an opinion. Decluttering is not to be rushed because speed won't allow us to take our decision-making to the next level.

We suggest you reframe your decluttering in a way that focuses on deciding what to keep rather than what to let go. Just that simple switch in perspective can be powerful. So when you've emptied a section of your wardrobe, begin by identifying your favourite items. These are the things you reach for again and again. These can be put back in your wardrobe as a starting point.

Then, once you have exhausted the simple choices, it's time to delve deeper and assess the items that you have never even considered decluttering before, and the ones you have considered but decided against.

You will be evaluating each and every item you have taken out of your wardrobe to determine its worth to you in the context of your current lifestyle.

We need to focus on emotions first, stuff second. For each piece of clothing, think about the following:

- Is this item something you will realistically wear soon?
- Do you have similar items to this in your wardrobe that you prefer and would choose first?
- Was this item a gift that you are keeping out of guilt?
- Are you holding on to the thought that you spent too much money on this item?
- Is there something about how this item looks on you that is stopping you from choosing it?
- Does this fall into the sentimental clothing category and can it be left until later in your journey (Chapter 12)?

Stick with it and trust the process because this stage is the hardest. This is where we are wrestling with habits we have had for years, so take your time. Ensure you feel in control and happy with each and every decision you are making.

Decluttering Category by Category

Once you have made your decisions about what to keep and what to let go, it's time to think about categorisation. What sort of categorisation is going to work for you? Do you have a tried-and-tested system, or do you struggle to keep on top of it? Do you want to maintain a simple system with sections for skirts, trousers, tops and jackets, or do you feel like you could go further still, for example by categorising your tops by sleeve length? Is colour coding the way forwards for you? Or could you store full outfits together? Does the way you have your folded clothes divided make sense today? Is there an equitable split between you and your partner if you're sharing your space?

The categories you can choose are endless and personal. Don't try to replicate a fancy-schmancy wardrobe structure you've seen on social media. Create a system that is going to make your day easier to manage and that is simple to maintain. That way, your wardrobe will work for you, rather than against you.

Storage and Organisation

Storage in a bedroom is often already established. We normally have a combination of hanging space, drawer space and shelf space, but is it working for you? We have a habit of following traditions that we learned growing up. If we grew up in a house where T-shirts were folded, we continue that tradition without really evaluating whether this works well for us now (in a completely different home with different rooms, storage, time and people).

If you are naturally more disorganised than organised, using hanging space works better. If you have an option to hang things that you haven't in the past, consider changing. You can hang jeans, T-shirts, even gym wear. Basically, folding involves more effort than putting something on a hanger and is much less forgiving. Now is the time to evaluate your current system and make some changes if necessary. Make sure all your hangers are facing the same way on the rail, as it makes for a neater look and helps accessibility.

If you have shelves, can you introduce some boxes to containerise things? Deep shelves in wardrobes can be tricky to keep tidy and stuff often disappears to the back of beyond, never to be seen again. If you introduce and fold clothes into boxes, you can easily see what you have by lifting the boxes out of the shelf when you need to grab something. These simple changes can reap huge rewards.

Shoes and bags are notoriously tricky to store and any storage you use is hugely dependent and bespoke to the space you have. Most people just have to find a sensible solution that works for them. If you are compromised on space, having less is always going to make things easier. Boring, I know, but oh so true.

If you have a bedside table, it often contains lots of bits and bobs, so use containers to subdivide. There are lots of containers available to buy, but plastic takeaway boxes and phone boxes you may have hanging around your home work perfectly too.

If you need to store things under your bed, use containers that are lidded and can pull out easily. The same goes for storage on higher shelves of wardrobes. Bedrooms get dusty so any box you use should be lidded.

When you have decided on your storage and organisation, it's time to reinstate things and put your items back in the right categories. Hang instead of fold if that's a decision you've made. Swap clothes over to a new hanger if you are going down that route. Start to fold into drawers if you love to fold. Basically, everything you are keeping now goes back into the wardrobe and drawers.

The Finishing Touches

While you may be impatient to get the job done, you still need to devote care and attention to the finishing touches. This is a stage that so many people miss, but it is vital to give you that feeling of accomplishment that is going to encourage and motivate you to continue with more decluttering in a different room. So, what do you need to do to get finished?

Ensure your bags for donation are situated ready to be sent to their next destination, whether that's straight in the car or ready for drop-off or pick-up in your entryway. Don't be that person who drives around for months with a charity pile in the boot of your car. If getting to a charity shop is a faff, put it in your diary and make it happen. If you have to return items to family or friends, send that text to initiate the process. If you have found items that need dry-cleaning, hand-washing or mending, work out when you'll do that task.

Then grab your vacuum cleaner and cleaning cloths and give the room a final once-over. Move anything you have found in the bedroom that belongs elsewhere to its rightful room in your home. Change your bedding as it will be dusty from all the activity, then take that 'after' photo!

TAKE A MOMENT

We're done! You can tick the bedroom off your list now and your decluttering muscle is definitely strengthening. Isn't it a great feeling of accomplishment? Make sure you take the time to enjoy the fruits of your labour and to reflect by considering the following:

- Can you feel a sense of calm now your wardrobe contains less and is more orderly?
- Do you know how many items you've decluttered? Are you surprised by the amount?
- Did you encounter any emotions you had not considered before?
- Do you think going through this process will encourage you to shop differently?
- Have you learned anything in the bedroom that is going to help you in other areas of the home?

7

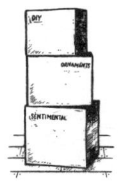

Indoor storage areas (lofts, attics, basements and storage units)

'Procrastination and clutter go hand in hand.'

It's now time to focus your decluttering attention on the outer reaches of your home. The place that houses a veritable treasure trove of all manner of stuff. A room where, within moments, you can flit from wondering why on earth you kept something for so long, to rediscovering something so precious that you're crying happy tears. A room that brings nostalgia and overwhelm in equal measure, and somewhere that you only ever venture into on a needs-must basis.

We are, of course, talking about indoor storage spaces. Depending on where you live, this may look like a loft or an attic at the top of your home, a basement or cellar at the bottom of your home, a designated storage room in the body of your home, or maybe even a storage unit away from your home. Whatever indoor storage space you have, the techniques in this chapter can be used for tackling them all.

If you are lucky enough to have storage space, then it's often the case that you can't begin to imagine how you would function without it. It's a real bonus to have a room where you can store things you need infrequently or love deeply but don't want in the main body of your home. But, more often than not, along with these useful and precious items, there's a whole heap of other stuff in there too – items that you *don't* use, need or love. These unnecessary items clutter up the space and stop it from being a versatile, practical storage area that enhances your life.

Let's talk about all that other random stuff. Half the time, we're at a loss as to how it even got there! If we're being honest, do we really need it, use it or love it or have we just forgotten about it? Have we just fallen foul of the 'out of sight, out of mind' mentality? Do we even know what's there? Are we really 'lucky' to have a room that is crammed to the rafters with stuff that is not serving us in our current lives? Yes, in principle, but we would be so much luckier if we treated our storage areas with the same care and attention as all the other areas of our homes.

Now, before we go on, we hope you're not feeling discombobulated. You might be thinking, 'But I don't want to do this room now. I want to concentrate on the living room and hallway and other areas that people will see.' If this is you, then we hear you. It might seem a little rogue to move into this indoor storage area now, when you have more pressing rooms front of mind, but bear with us. This process is all about building up your decluttering muscle step by step. Even though this may not be the area you *want* to tackle next, it's the one you *need* to tackle next – the one that makes most sense psychologically and practically. Let's explain.

Although tackling your indoor storage area might feel intimidating, it will provide the opportunity to make a big leap forwards in terms of evaluating your current life and what you need in it, which in turn will provide a great opportunity for you to hone your decluttering skills and further strengthen your decluttering muscle. Tackling your indoor storage space will also allow you to let go of significant volumes of stuff, which, in turn, will boost your motivation. Physically, it will create some space and order in your indoor storage spaces that can then be used to house things that may currently live in other rooms but could actually be stored in your less high-traffic storage space. And, actually, the decisions to be made in your indoor storage spaces can be much simpler than you might think because often you've actually already made some of them years ago (you just didn't know it at the time!).

So, strap yourself in for the ride. This is going to be fun!

The thinking

Emotional Preparation

DELAYED DECISIONS

We alluded to the fact that some of the decisions about items in your indoor storage spaces may have already been made without you knowing about them. This is because a storage area of this kind is a hotbed of procrastination. If there's one thing in life that's a given, it's that procrastination and clutter go hand in hand. Let us give you an example or two of what we mean by this.

You decided to replace the set of curtains in your living room five years ago but you kept hold of the old set in the loft because you're absolutely going to go back to your noughties decor choices at some point.

Or you took your old college textbooks off your bookcase 10 years ago and stuck them in the basement. They are still there – granted a bit dusty and you curse every time you have to step over them to get the Christmas decorations – but who knows when you might need your second semester seminar notes on *Romeo and Juliet*?

And then there's the kettle you replaced in your kitchen because it was past its best. Now it's got pride of place in your cellar in case of emergencies. You never quite know when your new kettle will break and your old battered one will be the only possible solution for your morning cuppa.

Do any of these examples resonate with you? I suspect you might even be laughing at yourself for having your own versions. What do all these examples have in common? Yup, you've guessed it: they're all examples of delayed decision-making.

The truth of the matter in all of these examples is that you made the decision years ago that an item was no longer serving you – you've removed it from your current, everyday life – but you weren't ready to let it go. So, off it went into an interim storage place, where you are holding it before delaying the inevitable.

So, for many items held in our indoor storage areas, we've actually already done the hard bit by deciding that the item is no longer worthy of its place in our homes. Recognising where procrastination is sabotaging our decluttering progress in this way is important because we can then learn to be more forthright in our decision-making moving forwards. (This will help us to avoid holding on to a build-up of things we are unlikely to ever use again!)

So, there's the good news. The fact that you already subconsciously made the decision years ago to move items into your storage space, coupled with the passage of time, means that much of this storage clutter becomes a no-brainer – an easy decluttering win!

LIVING IN THE PAST AND FOR THE FUTURE

Let's remember here that making decisions about the things you have chosen to store long term isn't *always* easy though. Sometimes we have delayed making decisions because we are sentimental about the past or the future. The curtains we mentioned earlier were the first ones we had when we moved into a new home. The college textbooks are a nostalgic reminder of our early achievements. The kettle we are keeping might be earmarked for our child in case they set up home and need a helping hand.

Sentimentality and practicality will always have a valid place in our homes and our hearts, but we need to exercise realism too and find the right balance. The nostalgia we feel about those textbooks isn't being enjoyed if they are stuck in a box. Are we really going to use up valuable storage space for those old curtains until they become vintage? And our child may not need or want all our hand-me-downs and would rather make their own choices about how their home looks.

It's vital to keep perspective. It can be too easy to keep things just because you have the additional space to do so. While the things in our storage areas will differ greatly to the day-to-day things we have within the body of our homes, we still need to keep the volumes under control and make the right decisions about whether something has become clutter. This is because our priority in our storage spaces, as within all areas of our homes, should be to keep the things we are using in the here and now.

Yes, it's worth allocating small areas of our storage spaces to honour the past and prepare for the future, but our homes should not be consumed by these things. So, while you are tackling this area, be mindful of prioritising the storage of things for your current life, and favour quality over quantity for anything else. Your future self will thank you for it.

SAFEGUARDING SENTIMENTAL

There will undoubtedly be an abundance of sentimental items in your indoor storage area. Your childhood swimming certificates, years of birthday cards, anniversary cards, wedding cards and condolence cards all bundled up together, artwork from your children that you just couldn't bear to part with, diaries and calendars that are decades old. It's the natural place to store them, right?

Actually, our preference would be that you bring sentimental items into the body of the home so you can see and enjoy them on a regular basis and get that warm fuzzy feeling inside. But we recognise that not every sentimental item is suitable to be displayed. Some items need to be kept for posterity, some for future projects, some for safekeeping, so a storage area is the natural spot for them.

Decluttering sentimental items is not a task for today though. Our decluttering muscle needs to be stronger to navigate the tough, emotional feelings we will encounter with these items, so we'll tackle them later, in Chapter 12. For now, as you work through your indoor storage areas, we would urge you to simply gather your sentimental items together (trying as hard as you can not to get lost in rediscovery), box them up safely, label them 'Sentimental items' and put them to the side to come back to later in the decluttering process.

'JUST IN CASE'

It's time to talk about keeping things 'just in case'. This emotion pervades cluttered homes everywhere and is a tough nut to crack. Our indoor storage areas are a catch-all for just-in-case items, so the time has come to dig deep and truly challenge our thought processes.

If we were to really ask what we mean by keeping something 'just in case', would we be able to truly articulate its future purpose? In most cases, probably not. This is because just-in-case items are often kept due to a sense of fear that throwing them away might be a mistake or to nervousness that our circumstances may change.

Those dining chairs we kept 'just in case' we ever decide to take up upcycling as a hobby. That rah-rah skirt we kept 'just in case' we ever decide to go to a fancy dress party that's eighties themed. You think you're all done with your family at three kids but who knows whether you'll want a fourth. You're pretty certain you don't want to finish that degree you started but who knows, you might. You think that dinner service you inherited has value but you're not sure. Uncertainty means we have a valid reason to hold on to things we may never need again. And often the things we are storing because of this uncertainty are big and bulky, such as prams, course notes and furniture.

So how do we navigate this type of unknown? Well, first we need to evaluate whether keeping these just-in-case items is compromising the space we have for the things we need for today. The less space we have to work with, the more exacting our decisions need to be.

We will need to focus on realism. How realistic is it that that uncertain thing is likely to happen and what would the consequences be if we didn't have the related item? Once your decisions become intentional (rather than fear-based), most of them will be the right ones,

However, it's very normal – when working through a lifetime of stuff – to accidentally let something go that you later discover would have been helpful. When this happens it's important to not allow it to be a setback. We need to be brave and confident that letting go of a surplus of items will allow us to find and cherish more important ones. Trust us, if you do have regrets about decluttering something (and it's a rarity), it's almost never a just-in-case item (it's almost always a sentimental item instead, but more on this in Chapter 12).

GARNERING GUILT

We're going to keep coming back to guilt over and over in each and every room in our homes. Guilt has a strong hold on us all, as it relates to three very important areas of our lives: money, aspiration and other people.

We keep things because we feel guilty that we spent (or even wasted) money on them and we therefore struggle to let those items go, because we feel that keeping hold of them will make us feel better. That exercise bike we bought on a whim back in 2010 when we were on a health drive. Three years with no miles ridden and the ironing piled on top means it was consigned to the basement. Realistically, it should have been donated or sold, but we felt guilty about both the money we spent on it and the fact that we didn't manage to achieve our goals, so it stayed.

We don't want to upset other people, so our indoor storage areas (and indeed other areas in our homes) are full of items that, although we have made a very conscious decision we don't want them (as we've removed them from the main body of the home), we can't quite bring ourselves to let go of them because of guilt. Relationships are tricky, and so are the decisions related to those relationships. Decluttering that painting your friend bought you that is just not to your taste isn't easy, so you stack it up with all the other old paintings in your storage area, where it's unloved, untouched and taking up valuable space. The guilt relating to other people's feelings and the ability to prioritise your own feelings takes time to navigate but when you rationalise it, it can be a powerful switch.

Decluttering and organising indoor storage areas can feel like a journey through time that will uncover a range of emotions. Our lives ebb and flow and so does our stuff. Don't forget your decluttering journey is comprised of a number of different projects that happen over time that lead to a process. And that process will be tweaked and fine-tuned for the rest of your days with each individual project you undertake. You don't need to transform your home in one fell swoop from being cluttered to clutter-free. This is not a race. Take your time, enjoy the things you find, look forward to what an organised home will mean for you and your loved ones. And remember, every item that you choose to let go of is a step in the right direction.

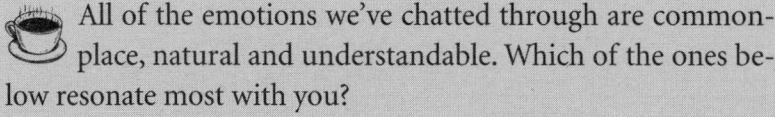

TAKE A MOMENT

All of the emotions we've chatted through are common-place, natural and understandable. Which of the ones below resonate most with you?

- Do you have things in your bulk-storage areas that you've already decided don't belong in your home but you just haven't taken the plunge to let go of?
- Are most of the things you are storing from a period of life that's long gone or earmarked for something that may or may not happen in the future?
- Are you guilty of keeping things 'just in case'?
- Do you have things you have been gifted or inherited and you feel as if letting go of them would be doing a disservice to the person?
- Or is your bulk-storage issue plain and simple: it's out of sight and out of mind, so it's slipped way down your list of priorities?

Goal Setting

BIG-PICTURE GOALS

Each room you work on in your home will have a different big-picture goal, all of which lead to your ultimate dream of a clutter-free, organised home. Now it's time to set your big-picture goal for your indoor storage space. Here are some ideas of what this big-picture goal might look like:

Making it easier to find things. We're taking things right back to basics here, but it's important. Indoor storage areas are so full of all manner of things that it can be difficult to find what you're looking for. If your partner asks you where something is and your response is 'in the loft somewhere' then what you need is organisation, labelling and zoning. We need to become more confident about what area of the loft or basement something is stored in. Ultimately, your goal is to save time and avoid frustration by creating order. For example, you may have a project in mind – family history, photograph organising or upcycling – and you know that what you need for that project is around, but it's buried somewhere. The goal of adding order to your indoor storage space can therefore be a great driver.

Making it easier to retrieve things. Often, because these storage areas are so full of stuff, it can be physically difficult to move things around in order to retrieve what you need. Indoor storage areas can be full of large boxes, heavy boxes, cardboard boxes, a mishmash of different sizes of boxes and rickety shelving, all of which is hard to navigate. So, your goal might be to make the space easier to manage logistically and physically in order to access what you need.

Preparing the space for an upcoming renovation project. One of the reasons we fail to give as much care and attention to storage areas is because these rooms are often unfinished. Maybe if it is a loft space, it isn't fully boarded or doesn't have a good, solid loft ladder. If it's a basement or cellar, maybe it doesn't have finished walls or still has a bare concrete floor with no covering. This often means there's a psychological barrier in place that makes it a less appealing space to be in, so we subconsciously choose to spend as little time in there as possible. And without investing time, we can't create order.

Just think of a space that you refurbished or decluttered recently. You have an additional impetus to keep it looking its best because it's a nice space to be in, and you're proud of it, so you invest additional time and energy there.

As these indoor storage spaces are incredibly useful, it's worth investing time and sometimes money into them so you can view and use them as a natural extension to the rest of your home. But often we can't imagine getting our spaces to a position where we could get a tradesperson to board out a loft or add some vinyl floor covering in a cellar because it's just too full of stuff. So, there's your goal right in front of you: you could focus on decluttering in preparation for renovating the space.

Determining your big-picture goal at this stage is vital, so even though you're chomping at the bit to get started, take just five minutes to think about what it is that is going to keep your momentum going. Write it down and keep it front of mind. Now there are just a few practical things to put in place and we'll be ready for the off.

Planning Section by Section

By now you know how important it can be to break down your projects into smaller, manageable chunks. An indoor storage area can vary from something compact to something extensive, and the types of items that you store there will vary hugely. You may also have more than one indoor storage area. So how you choose to break this project down needs to be determined by you after assessing the parameters and contents of your indoor storage area/s.

Please check the 'Decluttering questions' section on p. 118, which will give you examples of some broad categories to work within. Please do not skip this vital part of the process. Spend some time working out what sections feel achievable and sensible to you within the time you have available to devote to this project.

Physical Preparation and Logistics

First things first, layer up. Indoor storage spaces are often not heated or cooled so they can vary in temperature throughout the day. You therefore need to wear the right clothes, which you can put on or take off as needed. And shoes are vital too. Unfinished spaces have awkward surfaces, random nails sticking out here and there, and splinters threatening to pierce their way through your socks, so choose a comfortable, sturdy shoe.

If you're working in an area that is up a ladder or down some awkward stairs, you're not going to want to be up and down every five minutes, so do take time to grab water and snacks to keep your energy and hydration levels up.

Take all the tools you're going to need for the job with you: bin bags, labels, a vacuum cleaner, cleaning cloths. Have them all to hand so you can make as few journeys as possible.

And your poor body might be in for a battering. In indoor storage spaces we're often working on the floor, lifting heavy boxes in awkward spaces or banging our heads on low-hanging rafters. It's unavoidable, so do be ready for a few aches and pains tomorrow.

We're making it sound like we're going into battle! It's not that bad, but decluttering indoor storage areas does often require a little more physical effort than other areas in your home. So, if anyone has been thoughtful enough to offer help to you during your decluttering journey, now's the time to grab that offer with both hands. When it comes to the decision-making you may want to do that alone and take your time, but for the practicalities of lifting heavy boxes, moving them around in rooms that are tricky to manoeuvre, carrying things up and down ladders or taking bulky items out of the home for donation, if you have a helper then it can be a godsend. In fact, when it comes to using the ladder with heavy items it's a non-negotiable, otherwise you will be compromising your safety.

And finally, think about your exit plan. Depending on what you have up there, some of the stuff may require more than a bin bag. You might have furniture, old electricals, appliance boxes or old computer equipment. These things are heavy and your donation options might need thinking about in advance. The last thing you want is for half of your storage area to be sitting in your hallway for days or weeks while you work out what to do with it, so think about your exit plan before you start decluttering. A quick internet search or asking for advice on a local community group page should give you the information you need. If you require a van to collect your donations, have that pre-arranged before you get started, and if you need a skip or dumpster then have that on order too, so it's ready and waiting for you.

The doing

How and Where to Get Started

We've done the thinking, we've set our goals, we have all our equipment to hand, so let's take a 'before' photo and get started.

Now, most rooms in the body of our homes have a semblance of organisation and categorisation already in place, so it's a little easier to know where to start decluttering. Indoor storage areas may have some order to them, but more often than not, they are a little more chaotic!

If you can see your organisational structure, work using the categories listed on p. 124, but if your home is more chaotic, just get started. Clockwise, anticlockwise … you choose, but work your way systematically round the space. Try not to flit from one part of the room to the other or else you might lose track of where you've tackled. Decluttering and organising a storage space just evolves. It's all about taking things one box, one item or one shelf at a time, systematically, and pacing yourself.

Be mindful of your energy. You may be able to tackle a storage space like this in one session, but it's unlikely: it will probably span several sessions. In these kinds of areas it's easy to get lost in the moment as there's so much sentimental and nostalgic stuff lying around, so be sure to use those timers and take breaks.

Decluttering Questions

As we've discussed, indoor storage spaces hold a mishmash of items that fall into many different categories, so how do we make sense of what to keep and what to let go?

We have devised a set of questions to help you make decisions when decluttering your indoor storage spaces. They are listed below, ordered category by category, item by item. We suggest you familiarise yourself with this list beforehand, then keep it close as you declutter in case you need a handy reminder.

One last note before you start: we recognise that these questions are a lot to process, but that's the nature of a storage space. Some of the questions may not apply to you at all, some of them you may have worked through years ago, and others you may struggle with. The important thing is to establish that the stuff you are keeping is truly worthy of its place.

HAND-ME-DOWNS

- Are you ever going to use them?
- Do you need to have an honest conversation with yourself or the person who gave them to you?
- Will you ever put your child in something that is 10 years old?
- How certain are you that you'll have another baby to use the baby equipment you're storing?

CLOTHES

- Are you going to fit back into the clothes you are storing?
- Are you going to want to wear these clothes you are storing when you have newer versions?
- Is your rotation system for summer/winter clothes working?
- How long is it since you've actually looked at these clothes?
- Are you going to re-wear your old maternity clothes if you have another baby?

TOYS

- Will your kids want the stuff you are keeping for their kids?
- Is your toy rotation system working?
- Will you want to buy new ones if you have grandchildren?

FURNITURE AND PICTURES

- Are you ever going to put back up the pictures and photos you have taken down?
- Are you ever going to use those chairs you kept when you changed your formal dining room over?
- Are you ever going to get round to that furniture upcycling project?
- Will your daughter really want the desk from her childhood bedroom in her new home?

SEASONAL DECORATIONS

- Are you choosing to use each and every decoration you are storing each season?
- Have you sorted through the Christmas decorations recently and donated the excess?
- Are you still decorating the house as much as you used to now that the kids have moved out?
- Have your tastes changed over the years?

SENTIMENTAL ITEMS AND PHOTOS

- Do you need to put these sentimental items aside to tackle in Chapter 12 or have they recently already been sorted?
- Is the loft or basement the best place to store sentimental items and photos?
- Are you keeping items for the kids that they keep saying they don't want?

BOOKS AND NOTES

- Do you really need old course notes or work stuff?
- Is it really sensible to keep an overflow of books in boxes that you haven't looked at for years?
- Is the weight of these boxes of books excessive in this space?

PAPERWORK

- Have you got more archival tax stuff than you need legally?

- Do you even know what's in the boxes of paperwork?
- Can you now get the stuff you're keeping online?

SUITCASES
- Do you need to keep old suitcases that weigh almost as much as the airline's luggage allowance?
- Is it really necessary to keep hold of laptop bags from the noughties and briefcases that never see the light of day?

ELECTRICAL EQUIPMENT
- Is it time to take that hard drive out of that old computer and retrieve the information off it?
- Are you ever going to use that old printer?
- Is your old TV really nostalgic?
- Do you really need the 10-year-old appliance box for every piece of electrical equipment in your home?

CAMPING AND SPORTS EQUIPMENT
- Are you ever going to return to badminton and if you do, will you buy a new racquet?
- Do you choose to rent skis and boots and no longer need your old boots?
- Have you replaced some of this camping equipment with more modern, lightweight versions?

INHERITED ITEMS
- Are you keeping things out of duty to the person they belonged to?
- Are you delaying looking through these items because it's too emotional for you? If so, is this a sentimental item that you should put aside to consider in Chapter 12?

Organisation and Storage

As your indoor storage area project evolves it will start to become clear what type of things you have decided to keep. We start to see the volumes of things we have, what shape and size they are, how many of each particular item we have and whether the types of organisational systems and storage we have currently are working or not.

We then have some decisions to make. Do we need to introduce shelving if there isn't any? Are the boxes we have used historically up for the job or do we want to change them to something more substantial? For example, if we have historically been using cardboard boxes, are they still fully intact and the perfect solution or would plastic be better? If we have been using plastic boxes, do they have lids, do they stack, are they similar shapes and sizes? Are we interested in creating a storage area that is aesthetically pleasing? Do we have the budget to invest in new storage? If we do have money to invest in storage, would we rather allocate that budget to areas of the home that you see more often? Are you avoiding plastic for environmental reasons? There are so many variables to consider.

Every home is different, every storage area is different, every budget is different and every goal is different. But to steer you in the right direction, here are some things we have learned over the years when it comes to storage solutions that work a treat:

Favour boxes that close or have a removable lid. The things stored in your indoor storage areas are, by their nature, seldom used, so we need to protect them from the elements and insects.

Use lidded boxes that stack. The ability to stack is an additional bonus if you don't have or need shelving or racking. This is where having uniform boxes is a bonus. Stacking is so much easier if boxes are the same shape or size.

Measure shelves and boxes. It's important to always measure boxes if you'd like to ensure they fit on a certain shelf or to measure the shelf to ensure it works with your boxes, depending on what came first. Measure the height, depth and width of these items.

Avoid oversize boxes. The size of the box is going to be determined by the size and shape of the item that needs to go inside it. But do be careful not to restrict yourself to huge boxes that can be heavy and cumbersome and will have an impact on your desire to lift them up and down. If you are working in a loft space with eaves storage, shallow boxes work well and mean that you can maximise the full depth into the eaves.

Be mindful of the size of your loft hatch. Any boxes will need to be taken up or down, so invest in a wheel base. If you are working in a basement or cellar, it can be useful to raise the bottom box off the floor to protect it. Some box manufacturers make wheel bases that enable whole stacks of boxes to be raised off the floor and easily manoeuvred.

Colour-code your boxes. If you are going all out, it's possible to buy different-coloured boxes for different types of items for easy identification. A perfect example of this is for seasonal decorations: red for Christmas, orange for Halloween, for example. This elevates your organisation to a whole new level.

Each box needs a label. Don't stop at one label, either. These boxes are going to get moved around, so be sure to pop a label on the front, side and top of the box so you can see exactly what's inside from all angles.

Just a reminder: the functional cardboard boxes or plastic boxes that you have gathered over the years are absolutely fine. If it ain't broke, don't fix it, as they say. Rushing out to buy new storage is not the goal here. Creating an organisational system that is easy to use and that removes barriers is what this is all for.

Categorisation and Zoning

So, you've decluttered, you've put your chosen items into suitable boxes and you've labelled these boxes. Now it's time to zone your storage area into a space that is easy to use and will work for everyone in your household.

What do we mean by zoning? We mean that all the mishmash of categories we have spoken about need to be grouped together into similar areas that make sense logically, so you can find everything easily when needed. You may have categories that we haven't spoken about, but below is a list of the main ones we come across, and we suggest you create a separate zone for each of the following:

- Holiday decorations
- Seasonal sports equipment
- Photos, videos and slides
- Seasonal clothes waiting for rotation
- Hand-me-downs labelled by age category
- Toys that are in rotation
- Paperwork archives being kept for legal reasons
- Suitcases that are used for holidays
- Camping equipment
- Things being stored (temporarily) for others

And then to be put aside to tackle later:

- Sentimental furniture and pictures
- Memory boxes and sentimental items

You'll notice we haven't added a zone for books. That's because we truly believe that books should be in the body of the house ready to be enjoyed. Books in a box in the loft are almost never used again unless you have a very valid reason for storing them. I know you book lovers may be in violent disagreement right now, but it's harsh but true! (We're going to cover books in Chapter 10, so do hold off on this category for now if you are finding it difficult.)

The Finishing Touches

Once you've created your zones, move your boxes into them. Focus on easy access, where possible, by which we mean think about which items you will need to access more frequently than others. Make sure your labels are visible, add further labels to designate your zones, and you're almost there…

If you can use a vacuum cleaner in this area, be sure to give it a final once-over, along with a dust and a mop if possible.

Finally, create a zone map that you can put in the entrance to the room (a simple diagram in a plastic cover pinned up somewhere obvious will do). This means that everyone will know what goes where, and you can avoid being the only person who knows how to navigate your newly decluttered, freshly organised and meticulously zoned space.

Now it's time to take your 'after' photo and enjoy your sense of achievement.

TAKE A MOMENT

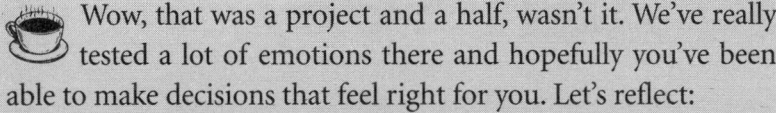 Wow, that was a project and a half, wasn't it. We've really tested a lot of emotions there and hopefully you've been able to make decisions that feel right for you. Let's reflect:

- Can you see the benefit of working in this bulk-storage area before tackling more visible areas of your home?
- Are you seeing the potential for storing items from other areas of your home now that things are a little more accessible?
- Are you happier, having finally made some tough decisions about items you have kept for a long time, just in case?
- Are you looking forward to being able to sort through the sentimental boxes you have uncovered once the more practical items have been dealt with?

8

Outdoor storage areas (garages, sheds and outhouses)

'There's no place in this journey for maybes.'

It's time to venture outside. Homes come in all different shapes and sizes and so too do outdoor storage areas. Whether you have a barn or a shed, a detached triple or a small, attached garage, the stuff that's stored in them and the emotions related to that stuff are common. We will be referring to this area as 'the garage' for ease, but the techniques can be applied to all outdoor storage spaces in whatever form they take for you. Now, it could be that your home doesn't have a garage or outdoor storage area and if that's the case, feel free to skip this chapter and jump straight to the hallway. (Having said that, it doesn't do any harm to furnish yourself with the full facts just in case your circumstances ever change!)

In days gone by, the garage was intended to be a home for your car but, more often than not in the 21st century, a garage houses more 'stuff' than it does vehicles. Your garage becomes an overflow for those things that don't fit inside your home and your poor old car gets relegated to your driveway or the road. Whether you want your garage to house a vehicle or not, it's well worth devoting time, energy and enthusiasm to creating an accessible, well-functioning space.

Many of the principles we have chatted through for decluttering your indoor storage areas (*see* Chapter 7) will be equally relevant now, and the stuff you have stored in both may be interchangeable. But there are still more factors to think about as we contemplate the diverse range of items that find themselves being stored in outdoor storage areas.

A garage, shed or outhouse is open to the elements, so cold, heat, humidity and damp are thrown into the mix of things we need to consider. Pests often take shelter in outdoor spaces and dust likes to settle. So, as well as factoring in our emotional connection to stuff, we have to think carefully about having the perfect storage solution to protect the stuff that we'd like to store there.

So why now? Why are these outside spaces on our decluttering agenda ahead of some of the internal areas of our homes? Our decluttering muscle is now well and truly flexed. We are able to make decisions more easily and we've looked carefully at some of the trickier logistical areas of our homes. So, it's now time for a morale boost and an increase in the volumes of items leaving our homes. Because a lot of the stuff in a garage is big, the opportunity for a marked, visible transformation is huge here, in the same way we were able to make huge breakthroughs in the indoor storage chapter.

In addition, a well-functioning garage or shed is another example of a space that can make or break the functionality and productivity of a home. This is because it is in these outdoor storage areas that we typically store the items associated with the 'extra-curricular' things in your life that bring joy – camping, sports, DIY, outdoor play, car trips, garden parties, for example – so it's more important than ever to get this space right. If finding the stuff to facilitate these occasions is too cumbersome, we will be less likely to plan them and, let's face it, being able to spend time doing the things we love is what this decluttering journey is ultimately all about.

We're asking you to validate the usefulness of your pastimes here, to unravel a lifetime of habit and potentially to work in an area that you have thus far been able to close the door on and forget. While these emotions are tough to work through, spending time doing so now will reap rewards later when we are feeling stuck.

Even though it's much nicer to declutter in the comfort of inside spaces, it's time to get geared up and venture into those areas that are up against the elements. We'll start analysing more closely what on earth is buried in there, so prepare for plenty of 'what was I thinking' moments as we get out into the fresh air and begin turning chaos into calm!

The thinking

Emotional Preparation

BREAKING DOWN BARRIERS

A garage is, by its nature, outside, so even if you have the nicest garage in the world, it's a bit less temperate than the rest of your home and involves effort to navigate to. And whenever additional effort is required, our subconscious mind sees and reacts to any barriers that stand in our way. Let's give a couple of examples.

You've finished a DIY project and you have things left over that naturally belong in the garage, but it's the depths of winter and so you run into your garage and just plonk them wherever is easy, vowing that you'll return tomorrow when it's warmer to put them away properly. But tomorrow never comes. Or you're just back from a day out with the kids, you know you need to put away the inflatables and cool box, but shifting stuff around to be able to fit these in feels a bit cumbersome, so you just dump it on the floor to tackle when you're not tired and haven't got grumpy children in tow.

The point is that there are numerous factors present in a garage that stop you from doing the right thing and taking action straight away: too cold, too dark, too many boxes to move or it's already too full.

Now, there isn't much we can do about the weather, but what we can do is make sure that we create a garage or shed system that is easy to work with. The easier the system, the more likely we are to use it. But to create an accessible, zoned space we need to first look at the stuff we have kept and assess whether it fits into our current lifestyles.

DELAYED DECISIONS

As we mentioned on p. 109, any bulk-storage area, whether it's inside or outside, is typically home to lots and lots of delayed decisions. Often, we have made a decision that an item no longer justifies its place in our homes, so we move it into a holding area (i.e. an indoor or outdoor storage space). We plan to return to it later, but later never comes and the clutter starts to build.

Outside storage areas are therefore full to the brim with delayed decisions. That 10-year-old wonky standard lamp from your hallway you replaced last year sits propped up behind the freezer. That appliance box you want to get rid of, but you know your partner won't be best pleased because they have a strangely compulsive thing about keeping appliance boxes. Those bags of decluttered items still sitting there waiting to be donated months later...

All these things start to build up. Before we know it, the garage is a dumping ground for things that we will never use. And this stands in our way of being able to easily find, use and return the items that we *do* actually want to use more frequently – i.e. the items that really add value to our lives.

Once you make a plan to analyse the things in your garage and their value to you in the here and now, the decisions to be made in the garage can actually be fairly simple. In fact, you're likely to wonder why on earth you even kept certain items in the first place.

THE MAYBE BOX

It's safe to say that when we go through our outdoor storage areas, we will undoubtedly find things we've not seen in a while. We may even see things we've purposely stored there so we can later return to make a decision about whether they should stay or go.

One of our real pet peeves when it comes to decluttering advice is the principle of setting an arbitrary timescale on something. We've all seen advice on social media and in magazines that says a simple way to declutter is to pop things you are unsure about into a box and date them for six months from now, then when the box is unopened six months later you will know for sure that you've not needed them. We think this is one of the worst pieces of advice you can follow. Let's break down why.

First, why should we adhere to a pre-prescribed six-month or one-year deadline? Who says that is the right length of time for us to personally determine we no longer need something in our lives? There are so many factors that come into play that determine when we are likely to use or need an item. We may not need an item again for years from now, but our decision to keep it may be intentional and therefore the item's place in our lives is justified.

Second, how can we truly evaluate whether or not an item is useful if it is stuck in a box out of sight (and therefore out of mind)? To truly evaluate an item's usefulness, we must ensure it is accessible and visible to us, particularly if it is an everyday item. If we keep these items in the body of our homes, we will be seeing them regularly and will have the option to utilise them as we go about our daily lives. This will help us assess more sensibly if something is of value to us.

Finally, one of the key parts of this decluttering journey, and the reason we are working through our homes systematically, methodically and thoughtfully is so that we feel 100 per cent in control of every decision we are making. We need to feel comfortable and brave enough to keep something if we are not ready to let it go. There's no place in this decluttering journey for maybes. It either stays or goes. Popping things into a six-month box takes us right back to the delayed decisions we spoke about on p. 109, which we want to avoid.

So, contrary to the oft-cited decluttering advice to throw it out if in doubt, we turn it on its head and suggest if in doubt, *don't* throw it out.

TO DIY OR NOT TO DIY?

A garage or shed is the natural spot to store tools, DIY stuff and other home improvement items. Now, there are actual DIYers, wannabe DIYers and never in a million years DIYers. It's so important to tap into that realism that is at the crux of any decluttering journey and make sure you have the appropriate number of tools and DIY stuff at home for the person that you are today and the projects you tackle.

Be honest with yourself. If something needs upgrading at home, are you going to tackle it yourself or outsource it to a tradesperson? If something gets damaged at home, are you going to repair or replace? Have you been an avid DIYer in the past but now have the funds to pay someone to do it? If a tradesperson comes to your home, are they really going to ask you to dig into your random electrical box rather than go to the store on their way to you to buy the exact thing they need? All these questions will lead you down the path of an honest assessment about whether you actually need all the things you are holding on to.

Tools, DIY stuff, paint, wallpaper, tiles – these are all found in abundance in a garage and nine times out of ten they never get touched. So why do we cling on to them?

The truth is we get nervous about issues (for example, bathroom tiles cracking, ceilings leaking, wallpaper getting defaced by a child) so we keep things in our garages just in case. Keeping the odd pot of paint for touching up or storing the last couple of tiles out of a batch isn't a problem, but what happens a lot is that these things are kept for an eternity. Paint pots that you open to discover contain just a dried-up inch of paint in the bottom, Superman wallpaper from your son's bedroom when he was nine (he's now 29), hand tools from back in the day before power tools were even a thing; they just don't justify the space they take up.

If you fall into the avid DIYer category, your assessment may be that you're going to use this stuff. But if you're not, it's time to be honest with yourself and your stuff.

MAKE DO AND MEND

If fixing things brings you joy or you make your living from your trade or passion, the chances are you'll have amassed associated stuff along the way. An offcut of wood, a unique tile fixing, a pot of varnish. You'll have an abundance of items that 'may' come in handy 'one day'.

Stuff that is doing 'no harm' to anyone. You have a treasure trove of bits and pieces gathered throughout the years and you love nothing more than finding the exact thing you need among your wares. So, what's the problem? Well, maybe there isn't one. If it's intentional, useful, well-organised and not stealing valuable space from items needed more frequently, it's absolutely not a problem.

We also need to be mindful that we may have inherited traits from our parents that are tricky to shift. Older generations lived, shopped and operated in a very different manner to the way we do in our modern lives. Screws, fuses and pieces of wood needed to be kept because they would be difficult to track down in a shop and potentially cost a lot of money. Nowadays there are very few things that can't be found and secured within a five-minute internet search. We have to weigh up the pros and cons of what we keep, determining whether it adds or subtracts value from our lives. There are no right or wrong answers; what you choose to do with the things in your home is a personal choice.

But what often happens is that this kind of collection becomes off-limits during the decluttering process. It's not subject to the same scrutiny as other things in your home, so things that have become clutter can get overlooked.

Recognising that you have a make-do-and-mend mindset is the first step to allowing yourself permission to delve into areas in your garage that you have marked as off-limits for years. And let's remember, working through a decluttering and organising project is as much about reconnecting with the things you own as it is about letting go of items you no longer need.

ACKNOWLEDGING ASPIRATION

Garages, sheds and outhouses are magnets for aspirational items. Working through this outside storage project provides the opportunity to re-evaluate these types of items and assess whether or not they deserve their place. This can be challenging though, as the things we are talking about here are often not easy things to let go of; saying goodbye to the item is like saying goodbye to the dream.

That treadmill you bought vowing this was going to be your year to focus on getting fit – how long has it been there? Even if the fancy took you to jump on the treadmill tomorrow, is it ready for action or is it stuck in a corner piled high with clothes?

That furniture you kept ready to 'upcycle' after seeing a project in a magazine. How long has it been waiting for you to get the time, the energy, the desire and the equipment to take this project to the next level? Has the passage of time made it less appealing, but now you feel guilty for not having followed through?

That car wax you are holding on to in case you decide to give your car an extra bit of TLC one day. Are you a DIY car valeting kind of person or are you a pop to the carwash and happily invest in someone doing it all for you person?

Aspirational thinking, and then feeling guilty that you have somehow failed in your quest to achieve something, rears its head in each and every space in our homes. The difference in a garage is that often the stuff in question is big, bulky and awkward, so letting the aspiration and guilt go can lead to big wins from a space perspective.

Operation Overflow

In some instances, having a space in the garage for overflow items may be necessary. For example, having regular access to a supermarket or store may be tricky for you because you live miles away or perhaps you are heavily reliant on other people to drive you there. Maybe money is tight, and you need to be very mindful of taking advantage of bulk-buy special offers. In these cases (or if you have another extenuating circumstance), you may need to buy more in one trip than you can fit in your kitchen, so having an overflow area for groceries, toiletries or other consumables might be necessary. That said, we want to urge you to evaluate whether this is truly required or if this has simply become a habit over time.

Typically, overflow storage spaces hold consumable items like food, products for cleaning, laundry or bathroom supplies. But often the overflow area is the last place you look for items when you run out, rather than the first. If you are edging towards owning 24 cans of marrowfat peas because you stocked up in 2018 when they were on offer, maybe it's time to start asking questions. If you have seven different window cleaning sprays and haven't cleaned your windows this year, it's definitely time to take stock. Embarking on a decluttering journey of your outdoor storage areas allows you the opportunity to reconnect with your things, to do an inventory of what you have, and to start slowly but surely shopping from home.

Shopping from home

What do we mean by 'shopping from home'? It means a systematic approach to ensuring you first use up what you have in your home before you add things to a shopping list. Sometimes that means some funky meal combinations or using a washing powder that's not your favourite, but boy oh boy is it satisfying to see your overflow go down and your shopping bill decrease along with it. We are big advocates of not wasting things that you can use up. Using up everything you have amassed over the years can take some time, but it's definitely worth the effort.

If you do need an overflow storage area for any reason, make sure you have a full picture of what is there and ensure you are topping up your cupboards with these older items before you add new. And then, if you do need to have an overflow section long term, this is where any new purchases will go.

And, again, we do suggest you consider whether your overflow storage area is a help or a hindrance. Are you constantly finding things that are out of date? Are you forgetting what you have when you shop? Have you just bought extra over the years out of habit? Most homes can operate perfectly well with no overflow at all. Maybe today is the day to make that change.

So, which of the emotions and habits we've mentioned in this chapter are wrapped up in the things in your own garage, shed or outbuilding? Take some time to consider the following:

- Have you identified any flaws in your outdoor storage area organisation that are stopping you from putting things away?
- Have you identified which of the emotions allowed you to make decisions about letting go of things that had outlived their usefulness?
- Are you clinging on to an idea of fixing and mending things yourself when you always use a tradesperson?
- Do you feel that you have a make-do-and-mend mindset that you will be able to overcome?
- Do you have a 'leave for six months then chuck' box?
- Is your overflow area overflowing?

Goal Setting

BIG-PICTURE GOALS

Having a big-picture goal in each and every space you tackle in your home is vital. The interesting thing about outbuildings is that often the big picture is to completely alter the space's purpose. Let's unpack that idea and look at some goals:

To bring your car off the drive or roadway so you can protect it, both from the weather and from theft or damage. If your garage is full to the brim with stuff, this is going to involve taking your decision-making and decluttering to the next level. Your goal will mean you have to make decisions that are likely to be more hardcore than you would typically feel comfortable about. It's a similar principle to downsizing. The space we have dictates the stuff we can keep. We may need to decide what we are willing to sacrifice to facilitate the big-picture goal of using this space for an entirely different purpose.

To create a space for a hobby or fitness. You may be committed to a fitness journey and your outbuilding could offer the space to house gym equipment. Keep that goal front of mind. Isn't it far better to have things in the garage that enhance our lives rather than detract from them?

To extend into the garage. If this is you, then you may need to remove every single item from this space so you can facilitate the extension. If that's the case, plough on with decluttering this space now using the skills you have learned so far, but accept that you may need to return for a 'Phase 2' later in your decluttering journey (as some of the things in your garage will need to be relocated to the inside of your home, where you will hopefully be opening up some extra space as you progress through this book).

To find what you need, when you need it without it being a huge ordeal. Maybe you want to put things away with ease when you need to. Simplification may be all you want.

So, what's your big-picture goal for your outdoor space? Whatever you choose, there's no doubt it will enhance your home and your use of this space. Your big-picture goal is going to be the very thing that you need to return to when the going gets tough. Once you achieve it, you'll feel that sense of accomplishment that allows you to keep on ploughing forwards in your decluttering journey.

So, over to you. Jot your goal down, keep it front of mind and let's put the foundations in place to make sure it happens.

Planning Section by Section

Take the time to look around your space and start to create a plan in your mind (or on paper) that is going to guide you section by section. You may already have some obvious delineation with shelving or racking. You may be able to start in one corner of the area and work clockwise. It may be sensible to tackle the floor first and wall areas next. It may be clear where you should start and how to progress, but try not to flit from place to place, so you feel in control of the process.

If you have no other option than to just go for it and wait for the project to unfold, that's fine too. Many a successful garage declutter has started in complete chaos and ended with beautiful calm. To help you with categorisation, take a look on p. 140 for a list of some common items found in an outside storage space.

Physical Preparation and Logistics

Decluttering and organising an outside space provides a unique opportunity for us to move things temporarily into a garden, patio or driveway so we have a larger area for gathering, sorting and deciding. This makes the process much easier logistically. If you're lucky enough to have a garden or a driveway that's secure, be sure to use it. You can take things out of your garage to clean the space before everything starts to go back in, but of course there are a few things to consider first.

THE WEATHER

If your outside space is on the agenda, try and pick a day when the weather is being kind. A few days beforehand, keep an eye on the forecast and earmark a day or a few days to devote to your endeavour. If the weather is changeable, a tarpaulin is a great way to temporarily cover things up to protect them from inclement weather or sun damage.

GETTING GEARED UP

Layers are king. When you're busy working outdoors, one minute you're freezing cold, the next you're roasting hot, so be sure to layer up. Wear the right shoes for the job, too, as there are often heavy, sharp and cumbersome objects in our garages ready and waiting to wreak havoc on our feet. If gloves make sense, grab them too.

And you're going to need brushes, cleaning stuff and heavy-duty bin bags, so make sure they're close at hand.

THINK OF YOUR EXIT PLAN

The things we find in a garage are unusual, so take time before beginning to declutter to find out what you can do with all those awkward items, such as flammable objects, electricals, paint and carpets. Some items can be donated to charity, some need to be recycled at your local recycling centre and some may require specialist treatment. Every area has its own rules for recycling though, so take some time to do this research in advance.

Sometimes a skip is the only sensible solution for your exit plan. But more often than not, it's overkill. By using your donation options and recycling centres, you can make sure your stuff is going to a worthwhile destination and there's no ambiguity. Skips are expensive and lead us down a path of throwing stuff into it that could have a second life. Only you will know whether a skip is required but it shouldn't be your only choice.

What we ideally need to avoid is having to put all the stuff that needs to be recycled or disposed of back into your newly decluttered outside space. At the very least, pop your unwanted items into your car, if you have one. It's even better if you can incorporate these runs to your recycling centre or charity shop into your decluttering session. If you don't have a car, try to co-ordinate so that the person or service that is helping you with your exit plan can be there in a timely manner on the day you are decluttering. You want to be able to progress without any barriers stopping you, so doing your homework about what goes where beforehand will be beneficial in the long run.

ASKING FOR HELP

We're going to be honest: while decluttering and organising an outside space is really satisfying and the rewards are huge, it can be a hard slog and feel never-ending. We've already talked about using a garden or driveway to extend the working area (where possible) to help logistically, but it's not sensible to leave things out overnight, so you're going to need to get as much done as you can in a short window of time.

We've also mentioned trying to get the stuff you want to declutter out of your home on the day of your project. Sometimes this may take several carloads, which will eat into the time you have available for decision-making and organising. The obvious answer here therefore is to ask for help. But it has to be the right help. You don't want anyone who's not on the same page as you derailing your efforts and undermining your decisions, so be sure the person who is helping is fully on board with your plan.

Asking your helper to be responsible for your predetermined exit plan is a brilliant solution. If they can take all the carloads to donate or recycle, that's going to allow you to stay focused on the task in hand.

Now the emotions are thought through, the goals are fixed, we're all geared up, so let's take a photo of where we are today and get started.

The doing

How and Where to Get Started

When considering how to embark on this area, you need to think about how much time and energy you have and whether it's likely you will be able to complete this whole task in one day. If you can, that will certainly make things easier, but that needs to be balanced against the possibility of you getting too tired and having to retire earlier than you would like. Here more than in any other area of your home, it is vital to be realistic about what you can do with the time and energy you have at your disposal.

Whether you decide to sort your outdoor storage area all at once or in stages, when you are taking things out, be sure to start to categorise them. Put all the bikes together, all the DIY stuff together, all the gardening stuff together, for example. The most important thing is to gather similar items like with like.

If you see a no-brainer decision (for example, something that is broken or not fit for purpose), put it in a designated donate/recycle area there and then. But if you need to take your time to truly analyse an item, put it with its friends and come back to it later.

If you have the luxury of being able to take everything out of the outside space and have done so, now is your time to turn your attention to cleaning. Start high and try to tackle dust and cobwebs and then end with the floor. If you have shelves, give them a wipe and if you feel you'd like to move your shelves around, go for it. You can always fine-tune this later, but it's good to look at any systems that haven't been working for you at this stage. As you work in this space you'll undoubtedly need to clean again later, but at least you are starting with a great foundation.

If you can't take everything out of a space at once, and have to instead work category by category, look for big wins that you are able to declutter first, such as large cardboard boxes, bulky sports equipment, bikes that are no longer needed, and take it from there. In all honesty, there's no magic formula for this one, you just need to go for it!

START EARLY

We're all about breaking things down into smaller, manageable chunks, but sometimes you just have to get stuck in and prepare for a longer day, and working through your outside storage space is one of those times. Start early to allow yourself ample time to take breaks and stay fed and watered throughout the day.

Decluttering Category by Category

An outside storage area houses all manner of things. Over the years of working in these spaces, we've identified several categories of items that are commonly found there. Some of these categories deserve their place, some categories need to be questioned and other categories are absolute no-brainers that should be on that donation pile without giving them a second glance.

Typical categories found in outdoor spaces include:

- Garden tools and equipment
- Outdoor living items
- DIY stuff
- Old paint and wallpaper
- Bikes and scooters

- Barbecues and their paraphernalia
- Ski, snow and sports gear
- Car maintenance supplies
- Old furniture
- Seasonal decorations
- Suitcases
- Camping equipment
- Old appliances
- Appliance boxes
- Outgrown or rotated toys
- Clothes
- Archival paperwork
- Memory boxes
- Photos
- Overflow food and cleaning equipment
- Exercise gear
- Top boxes and roof racks

We could go on, but you get the gist – it's a lot!

And because it's such a lot, we need to make sense of these categories (and the items within them) by editing them down to ensure we keep the best and ditch the rest. To help with your decision-making, we've come up with a list of questions to ask yourself about the items in your garage.

The questions that follow are listed category by category, to make things easier. It can feel overwhelming to see so many questions, so keep your mind firmly on your big-picture goal, take things one category at a time, schedule in those breaks and do the best you can.

We recommend that you familiarise yourself with these decluttering questions so you know in advance the kinds of emotions that will come up, then keep them to hand as you work category by category. This is not an exhaustive list, but you will be able to recognise patterns that you can use with other categories of items that are unique to you. The reasons why we keep things in our outdoor spaces is extensive and all our homes have different factors to consider.

Use the questions below to help guide you towards what items to keep and what items to declutter.

GARDEN TOOLS AND EQUIPMENT

- Do you actually maintain your own garden, or do you employ someone who brings their own equipment?
- If you bought something years ago to fix an issue, are you ever going to go back to an old product that's past its best or will you buy new if the problem reoccurs?
- Will you ever reuse the pots that came with the plants from the garden centre that are now in your garden?
- Do you have multiple tools of the same kind and do you have a preference for which to use?

GARDEN FURNITURE AND CUSHIONS

- Are all the outdoor cushions fit for purpose?
- Have you bought replacements that you prefer?
- Do you use all the candles, lanterns and ornamental stuff or are they aspirational?
- Is it the best use of your space to keep extra chairs for a party you may or may not have?

DIY TOOLS AND EQUIPMENT

- Does your tool collection reflect the jobs you're willing or able to undertake?
- Are you keeping an abundance of tools that have been handed down for nostalgic reasons? (Can you make a quick decision about these now or do these need to be put aside to be considered with sentimental items in Chapter 12?)
- Does the passage of time mean you have newer and better tools available to help you with a project?
- Has the tool collection been broken down into categories or is it something that needs to be decluttered and organised by someone else in your household?

OLD PAINT AND WALLPAPER

- Does the paint still exist on a wall in your home? Is it clear which room it's for?
- Is it congealed or past its best?
- Is the wallpaper in good enough condition should you need to use it?
- If the paint or wallcovering gets seriously damaged, would you claim on insurance and/or redecorate the room from scratch?

BIKES

- Are all the bikes age appropriate and in use by a member of your family?
- Are the bike tyres pumped up and ready to go?
- Do you have lights or other bike equipment that you no longer use?
- Are the bikes or scooters obstructing your access to frequently used items?

BARBECUES

- Do you have more than one barbecue?
- Do you use all the tools you have amassed over the years?
- Would you ever return to that disposable barbecue you bought on a whim?
- Are the briquettes you have fit for purpose?

SNOW AND SKI GEAR

- How long is it since you have used this snow or ski gear?
- Are you still actively pursuing snow or ski activities?
- Have you replaced ski equipment and kept hold of the old stuff?
- Can you still fit into the boots, snowsuits or ski wear?

CAR OR VEHICLE EQUIPMENT

- Do you clean your own car or take it to a car wash?
- Do you have manuals and vehicle parts for something you no longer own?

- How old is the oil you have kept to top up your car?
- Can you actually use those headlight bulbs or windscreen wipers now?

OLD FURNITURE

- Are you ever going to restore or upcycle that piece of furniture you inherited?
- Will you ever decide to put back into your house a piece of furniture you decided to take out?
- Does the furniture you thought might be useful for garage storage actually work for the items you need to store?
- Are those old paintings ever going to go back on the wall?

SEASONAL DECORATIONS

- Did you check your seasonal decorations last time they were in use to assess their usefulness?
- Are your storage boxes fit for purpose and optimised?
- Do you still decorate for every celebration?

SUITCASES

- Do you need all the suitcases you have kept?
- Are the suitcases available for use or full of clothes or other items?
- Do you need old suitcases that are too heavy for airline travel?

CAMPING EQUIPMENT

- Are there any pieces of equipment that you bought and didn't deliver what you expected them to?
- Have you replaced a smaller or older tent with an upgraded one?
- Is everything cleaned down and ready for use?

OLD APPLIANCES

- If the item you chose to replace broke, would you actually revert to this one or buy new again?
- How likely is it that that emergency you are keeping the appliance for is going to happen?

APPLIANCE BOXES

- If you move, will you be happy to hire a moving company and use their wrapping and boxing?
- If this appliance is faulty, is it essential to have the box to return it?
- Have you just got into a habit of keeping appliance boxes?
- If the appliance had to be built, can you actually get it back in the box?

TOYS

- If these toys have been deemed surplus to requirements, will the children or grandchildren ever return to them?
- If you are using a toy rotation system, is it working?
- Are you keeping old toys for nostalgic reasons, and would your own children want them for their kids?

ARCHIVAL PAPERWORK

- Is this paperwork decluttered, organised, categorised and in appropriate storage?
- Do you know that you absolutely need this archival paperwork?
- Can this archival paperwork be stored in the body of your home?
- Can you use a digital system for your archival storage?

STUDY NOTES AND WORK PAPERWORK

- Do you need to keep course notes from years ago? Are you ever going to look back at the content?
- Are you authorised to have some of the work-related documentation you have?

ITEMS WAITING TO BE DONATED

- Are you sure of exactly what is in these bags?
- Do you have a plan as to when they are going to be donated?
- Are they to be sorted through at a later stage in the process?

SENTIMENTAL ITEMS AND PHOTOS

- Is this outside space protecting your precious things?

- Have you favoured quantity over quality?
- Are you holding on to things for your children when they clearly don't want them?
- Can any of these sentimental items be brought into the body of the home and enjoyed?

Categorisation and Zoning

Zoning in your space is an important part of the process because giving something a logical home will ensure you instinctively know where to find it.

We will undoubtedly have been concentrating on gathering like with like into categories while we have been decluttering, so we've given ourselves a great head start when it comes to thinking about categorisation and zoning. But now it's time to fine-tune this, first by thinking through what's worked and what hasn't in the past. Things can always be improved, so take each category in turn and consider where might be an appropriate zone for it within your storage space. A logical system will start to unfold.

Our zones will be similar to those in our indoor storage areas and the key factors to consider will again be accessibility, visibility and logic. For a refresher on this, it might be useful to revisit p. 123.

Some of the categories we will include here ideally would not be in an outdoor storage area of your home due to variations in temperature, damp or pests, but sometimes it's the only option. Decluttering and organising your home involves compromise and we often have to store things in areas that are not the optimal choice.

Item zones that belong in outdoor storage areas include:

- Sports equipment
- Bulky household items
- Gardening equipment
- Outdoor living equipment
- Barbecue equipment
- Outdoor play equipment
- Car maintenance equipment

- DIY equipment
- Extra paint, tiles, flooring
- Bikes and scooters
- Roof racks and top boxes
- Camping equipment

Items that may be stored in an outdoor storage area (if no indoor storage space exists for them) include:

- Rotated toys
- Paperwork archives
- Suitcases
- Seasonal decorations
- Arts and crafts
- Memory boxes

You will see we haven't included a category for books and clothes in this list. This is because we truly believe that if these categories are going to be used in the right way then they should be in the body of your home. (We've already talked about clothes in Chapter 6 and we will be talking about books in Chapter 10.)

Organisation and Storage

By this stage, you've done the tough part of deciding what to keep and what to let go, and you've also had a chance to think about what zones you need in your space, so now it's time to look more closely at storage and organisation.

Many of the principles of organisation and storage in an outdoor storage area mirror those that we have worked though in our inside storage areas in Chapter 7. But for ease we will repeat the most important factors here, and add in other things to consider that are outdoor specific, too:

Introduce shelving and racking. Using shelving means that we don't need to keep moving boxes at the top of a pile to get to those at the bottom. Shelving and racking can be a game-changer and can be introduced gradually depending on budget. Be sure to think about the weight, height, depth and width of your shelving or racking when it comes to your purchase. Spending time on analysing dimensions now will save you frustration later.

Measure containers and boxes if you need to buy them. Be sure to measure the stuff that needs to go into them, too, to make sure you optimise what can fit. Take into consideration the weight of the items as well. Don't buy boxes that are too large, as this can lead to overfilling and make moving and handling the boxes dangerous. When it comes to outdoor boxes, buy the best storage you can afford as it will be around for decades.

Use lids for things that need to be protected and keep boxes unlidded and open for things that don't. A lid can be a barrier that stops us from easily and quickly being able to put something back into its home. Things like paint, tools, car cleaning stuff and gardening stuff is, by its nature, used for dirtier jobs, so a bit of dust here and there is not going to affect its usefulness. Boxes containing these items can therefore be unlidded. Boxes without lids work best if they are stored on open shelves and you don't need to stack them. But you're going to need a lid for things that will be damaged by the elements or that need to be kept very clean, for example yoga mats or arts and crafts supplies.

Use a wheelbase, which allows boxes to be raised off floors and moved around easily. It also safeguards against damp. But if you don't have a wheelbase, putting boxes directly on the floor works perfectly well too, or you can stack lidded boxes on top of each other on your shelves or racking.

Utilise roofs and walls. Bikes can go on walls. Gardening tools can be hung up on nails and hooks to keep them off the floor. Look around for innovative options for hooks, shelves and racking that will open up the option of vertical storage. Don't restrict your storage to the floor; walls are just as helpful.

Use a bike rack. In a garage, this can really help keep bikes and scooters upright. It also makes them easier to wheel in and out if they have a designated spot and will avoid you having to move other bikes to get to others. Remove those barriers!

Use large, round bins for balls and outdoor toys.

And as always, label, label, label; the bigger the better. Add labels to all sides of your containers and on to your shelf fronts. This is particularly important in outdoor spaces because these tend to be less well-lit and are used less often and by multiple people. A label will help with all of these factors.

The Finishing Touches

You've done it – we bet it feels so good. There's something strangely satisfying about decluttering an outside space. As we mentioned right at the beginning of this chapter, the stuff that is in there is typically to enhance your home or your well-being, so being able to find it easily and without hassle is so important.

But it's not easy. We're sure you are ready for a breather before you embark on the next step in your decluttering journey. You've been lugging around heavy boxes, making decisions about things that have been hanging around for years if not decades, and have no doubt made endless trips to take your unwanted things to be donated or recycled.

You may have enlisted a family member or friend to help you. Let's recognise that while that has no doubt been a huge help logistically, it can sometimes take its toll emotionally as you both get tired and fed up.

Before we move on from this project completely, let's revisit that zoning. Do the plans we had before we started to put all the puzzle pieces of organisation together still make sense? Are we able to keep all the categories together in the zones we had in mind, or do we need to compromise and amalgamate some?

Take time to really evaluate whether you have optimised the storage. Consider whether you have boxes that need to be replaced or generally whether anything is missing from your outdoor storage area masterplan.

Once you're happy with your zones, create a zone map. This can be a simple annotated diagram on a piece of paper slotted into a plastic cover and put in a prominent place near the entrance to your outdoor storage area. If there are other people in your household, explain the new system to them and reiterate how important it is for them to use the systems you have created.

Grab your cleaning cloth or brush and give the area a final once-over. Then take an 'after' photo and pat yourself on the back for a job well done. If you need to go and lie down in a dark room to recover, we hear you. Rest up, marvel at your accomplishments and soon you'll be ready for more of the feel-good feeling that decluttering brings!

TAKE A MOMENT

 Take a moment to think about what lightbulb moments working on your outdoor storage area has uncovered for you:

- Do you think the zoning of your outdoor storage will help you in the future? How?
- Do you feel like your decluttering muscle is building up with each area you tackle?
- Do you feel like you need a break before you move on to your next area or are you raring to go?

9

The hallway

'Done is better than perfect.'

Our home should be a sanctuary. A place where we can escape from the outside world. A place to relax, enjoy leisure time and take refuge from what life throws at us. Crossing the threshold from the outside world to your own personal space should be a positive experience. Putting your key in the door should be your subconscious signal that a change in pace is coming. You deserve an opportunity for relaxation and your hallway or entryway needs to be welcoming enough to facilitate that transition.

Now, whether you enter your home via a front or back door, you are likely to have a spot where you kick off your shoes, take off your coat and unload the day. This should be the place where you immediately breathe a sigh of relief, and that can mean things landing where they drop and staying there till they are next needed. A hallway can be a clutter hotspot and keeping it in check takes real effort at a time when we have the least energy to give.

Now, we don't linger in a hallway. Its purpose is transitory: to move from outdoors into the hub of the home. But that doesn't mean it should be ignored. On the contrary, a well-functioning, welcoming hallway can make or break your mood. It can turn that sigh of relief to a pang of anxiety in a heartbeat.

Your hallway is also the place where others have a window into your world. A knock at the door by a delivery driver, a neighbour or a friend allows a cursory glance into your hallway, where an impression is formed and a judgement is made.

So, what constitutes a hallway or entryway for the purpose of this chapter? Well, this space for you could be as small as a couple of coat hooks next to your door or it could be a space large enough to house a grand, sweeping staircase. We'll be pitching this chapter somewhere in the middle, as always. Some of the things we talk about won't be an option for you if you have next to no hallway, and if you have a large hallway (with plenty of storage) then you may not have a clutter issue at all. However, as always, the thinking and the doing discussed here are transferable to other spaces in the home. So, even if the items discussed here cannot be found in your hallway, they are very likely to exist somewhere.

Often the difficult bit of a decluttering and organising project is the emotions-based decisions we need to make that will lead to us parting with our excess. But in a hallway, as well as determining what to let go of, we need to configure the space to facilitate form and function. We need to hone our organising and categorising skills to make this area work like clockwork because there are constant ins and outs of items. If you are tight on space or the space you have to work with is awkward, this can be a challenge, but the good news is that your decluttering muscle is now at a place where, with our guidance and ideas, it's a challenge you will be more than able to conquer.

Once you have gone through the process of decluttering and organising your hallway or entryway, you will need to devote time each day to tidying it. These spaces are high-traffic areas, which take effort to maintain.

We're currently working in the peripheral areas of our homes. We've spent a while looking at storage spaces and now we're looking at entryways. It pays to create a functional, welcoming space that means coming home is a positive experience rather than one that leads to more stress. We'll be circling back to your living spaces very soon.

The thinking

Emotional Preparation

THE JUDGEMENT JUNGLE

As we've touched on before, one of the biggest issues we face when we have lived with clutter is other people's judgement. Wouldn't life be a whole lot kinder if we didn't have to deal with this? Judged as a child by our parents for being messy and then, in reverse, judged by our children for having a home they don't feel lives up to the standards of their friends' houses. Judged by our partners for not being able to get the basics of homemaking right and judged by friends who want to help but still manage to make us feel ashamed.

And it doesn't even stop there. Even though people don't vocalise their judgement, we can feel it from people who knock on our door to deliver a parcel, from our online food order delivery driver walking through your home to take the crates into your kitchen, and from the person who has come to fix your boiler. You sense their eyes darting around your hallway all too acutely.

We also feel a sense of judgement from people who have never even been to our homes and have no insight into our lives but might make sweeping and derogatory statements on social media about people who live with clutter. Although those comments are not about us, they feel personal.

Whether it's people entering our homes or commenting from afar, these judgements land harshly, we are hyper-aware of them, and they can be soul-destroying. We feel exposed, embarrassed and ashamed.

But the greatest judgement of all comes from ourselves. Years of judgement from others inevitably leads us down a path of self-criticism. We question why decluttering is such a difficult process for us, why we feel an irrational fear of throwing something out, and why we can't just get the job done like everyone else.

Trying to remove the shame we feel about our clutter doesn't happen overnight. It takes time, energy and effort to turn a corner and we need to be patient and tread our own regenerative path.

The good news is that the judgement of the parcel delivery driver and the darting glance from the neighbour can be removed from your world by focusing on the organisation in your hallway. How nice would it feel to be able to open your door without fear of judgement? It might not be the primary goal, but it would be a fantastic boost.

PREVENTING PROCRASTINATION

Many of us lead increasingly demanding lives with jobs to do, families to feed, loved ones to care for – and that's before we try and fit in a social calendar! It can sometimes feel like we're on the hamster wheel of life and, more often than not, we're exhausted. So, the last thing we may want to do when we get home, tired after a long day, is tidy up after ourselves and others.

Therefore, the truth is that many of us choose to procrastinate over 10-second jobs when we enter the home (not putting shoes away or deciding to step over the post rather than picking it up, for example – sound familiar?), even though these little jobs would actually save us oodles of time later. But, instead, we make that mental shift into relaxation mode as soon as we come through the door, even though a smidgeon of extra time in work mode would pay dividends.

Maybe you're rolling your eyes and thinking, relaxation? What relaxation? When you get home perhaps it's only just the beginning: there's dinner to be cooked, laundry to be done, homework to be monitored and more emails to be sent. You may feel there's no time to tidy up after yourself when there are so many other jobs to be done.

Whatever your version of getting home looks like though, there's a good chance that it doesn't include taking the time to put your shoes neatly in your shoe rack or spending a moment to recycle your junk mail and hang your keys carefully in their designated spot (so you can find them within seconds when you need them next!).

Reversing our tendency to procrastinate on entering the home takes time, but it is possible. Simple processes and adaptations can be made to help with this and set you up for success, such as ensuring you have a sensible shoe rack that is easy to use, a key area with hanging space for all the family keys or a designated spot to put the mail until you have time for life admin.

Form Versus Function

If you're not familiar with what form versus function means in the context of a home, let's clarify. Form is making a room or space look appealing, and function is making it work practically. We've already mentioned the importance of a hallway being welcoming when you come home. That's where form comes in. But we also need to make sure we have ample space to hang coats and store shoes too, which is what we consider function.

In an ideal world you would have the perfect combination of both in an entryway, but ultimately function should prevail every time. This is because having processes that mean you can easily put things away when you enter your home and easily grab things when you leave is key. It's therefore important to make sure that everything has a designated spot and that the chosen spot is fit for purpose. In addition, we need to be sure that your storage is optimised and that everyone is up to speed with what goes where. A hallway is prime real estate in a home, so its potential should be fully maximised.

You see, you can have the most beautiful decor in the world, but if your hall is overwhelmed with lots of clutter your eyes will never be able to move past the chaos. That designer coat rack you saw in a store looks beautiful with one carefully curated umbrella and a trench coat on it, but can you even see it when you have 10 coats all precariously hanging on top of each other? Those ornaments on your hallway console table look wonderful until your unopened post, your keys and your kids' bookbags are all piled up next to them.

Only when we've got the functionality right in the hallway can we turn our minds to form. Both are possible but, when it comes to creating a stress-free home that saves your precious time and energy, function wins every time.

Micro-organising

Pretty much every hallway around the world has two things in abundance: coats and shoes. Creating a system to keep these under control is vital. As always, the success of the system starts with having less. The fewer coats and shoes we have then the more easily we can maintain them. Rotation is going to play a part too. Not every coat and shoe we have needs to be in the hallway all year round, so your system may involve moving things into bedrooms or storage areas.

Coats and shoes are a clutter problem in most people's houses, which is why there is no shortage of suggestions on how to store them. Before we jump into buying storage solutions that promise to change the world though, we need to exercise caution. We need to favour function over form, as we mentioned above, but we need to tap into our own realism too. Function and realism combined equals success. Function without realism leads to micro-organising, which is something we definitely want to avoid.

What do we mean by micro-organising? As mentioned on p. 62, micro-organising is where a great deal of effort is required to maintain a system. Let us give you an example. You are a family of four with two gorgeous but boisterous under-sixes. As much as you'd love the kids' shoes neatly placed, it looks like Armageddon by your front door most days. You find a shoe rack and think it's the perfect answer. But it involves them (let's be honest, most likely you) placing these shoes carefully on the rack each day. Because it's so much effort it doesn't get done. This is a classic case of form without realism.

However, once realism kicks in, you can forfeit the 'perfection' of the shoe rack, grab a large basket and use that instead. It's easier for the kids to manage and, even if they aren't on board, it's simple for you to throw the shoes in for them. Using a basket to containerise a neatly grouped set of like with like items looks intentional and simply works. It's a system that sets you up for success because it's based on function and realism.

Now, we are not saying that micro-organising doesn't work. Some people love spending care and attention dotting the Is and crossing the Ts when it comes to their homes, but we need to make these changes gradually and ensure the other people in our households are on board with our new systems and processes, too. Tapping into realism combined with function, and constantly evaluating new systems to ensure they are workable for everyone, will make new habits a breeze.

The Value of Visibility

A hallway can be a real clutter hotspot, particularly if you have a table, a dresser or a sideboard near your door. Not only do we find ourselves plonking stuff on it when we enter the house, but we also put stuff on it to 'remind' ourselves of things that need to be taken with us next time we leave.

That pile of library books that's overdue, that dry-cleaning that's now hidden under the coats, those letters to post. We put them in what we believe is an obvious place, so they are visible to us. If you see it, you'll remember to do it, right? Sometimes this can work but often, if we don't have our clutter and resets under control, those 'to-dos' can find themselves sitting alongside other clutter, languishing on the hallway table for days if not weeks.

It's important to evaluate whether the system of leaving 'to-dos' by the door works for you. Is that visibility enough to prompt you to do the job itself or is the process broken? Visibility is so helpful, but we need to create a system that is intentional and gets results.

The Sweep Bag

It's time to introduce you to the sweep bag. What exactly is a sweep bag? Well, imagine the scene. Someone calls you to tell you that they're popping over in 30 minutes. You go into panic mode, your house is chaotic, but you *know* you can make it look vaguely presentable if you start skimming things off surfaces. So that's what you do: you grab a bag or a box and you 'tidy' up those areas of your home that your guest is likely to see. If it's out of place it goes in the bag: paperwork you want to tackle but haven't got round to; coins you emptied out of your pocket; hand creams you use every day; snacks you've grabbed from the kitchen; umbrellas you put down to dry; books you need to return to the library; crosswords you haven't finished. You get the drift… Those random bits and bobs cluttering up the house that hang around, more often than not, in your living room or kitchen.

We're in the hallway chapter so why are we talking about things from a living room or kitchen, you ask? Because the hallway is often where sweep bags end up. Out of sight, out of mind and in a hallway cupboard. We do the sweep, the room looks guest-ready, we throw the sweep bag into the cupboard, we vow to go back to it, but later never comes. Then, when we delve into the hallway cupboard months, or maybe even years, later we find our sweep bags and in them all manner of things we thought were lost. We may have been searching for the items for weeks or, even worse, we may have rebought them.

A sweep bag is the curse of a cluttered home, but don't worry, once you have established a place for everything and mastered better habits of putting everything back in its place, the sweep bag will be a distant memory. But, in the meantime, we must acknowledge the sweep bag's existence and do our very best to eradicate it as a decluttering and organising fix.

TAKE A MOMENT

The habits and emotions prevalent in the entryway to your home can make or break the success of your day or the vibe of your evening. So, make this part of your decluttering journey count.

Of the emotions and habits we've discussed, which sound familiar to you?

- Would your hallway look amazing if it weren't knee-deep in the detritus of daily life?
- Do you put off five-minute jobs that would save so much time later?
- Do you feel a surge of embarrassment every time the doorbell rings?
- Do you have a pile of 'reminders' by the door?
- Are you guilty of the 'sweep'?
- Do you love micro-organising when you have bigger fish to fry?
- Do you not devote sufficient time to your daily resets?

Goal Setting

BIG-PICTURE GOALS

Every area of your home that you tackle as part of your decluttering journey needs a big-picture goal. So, let's give you some idea of big-picture goals in an entryway that might resonate with you:

Time-based goal. You may want your hallway to have everything you and your family need to hand for a stress-free start to the day. You want to avoid that last-minute scream fest in the morning when everyone's trying to find gloves, PE bags, homework and water bottles.

Space-based goal. You have a fantastic area that you know could be used as an incredible boost to your storage solutions in your home. However, your entryway is currently crammed to the rafters and trying to find what you need is like wading through treacle.

Emotions-based goal. You may want to enjoy opening the front door when you come home after doing your chores or work for the day. Clearing the clutter means that your welcome home will be pleasant. This is a simple big-picture goal but it's hugely impactful on your well-being. Going even deeper into your emotions, maybe you'd like to remove that moment of embarrassment when you open your door to a guest, and they have a window into your chaotic world.

All of the above. You just want your hallway to function as it should – a clear and calm entryway to and from your home.

It's time to determine your big-picture goal. What is it about this space that needs to change? How will decluttering and organising your hallway impact your life for the better? Be specific rather than general, jot your thoughts down and let's make this happen.

Planning Section by Section

It's fair to say that hallways come in all different shapes and sizes. So, before you get started, take 10 minutes and have a good look around. What are we dealing with here? Is it an overflowing coat rack, an out-of-control shoe mountain or piles of post that are breeding? Do you have an understairs cupboard or a large cupboard that is part of your entryway? If you're lucky enough to have more than one entryway to your home, include them all as part of this project. This entryway project might be achievable in one day or it might take several days.

Spend some time thinking about how you can break this project down. Which elements can stand alone as individual projects? Which parts of your hallway will create the most scope for big wins? Can you do all the coats together, then all the shoes together, then your console table or sideboard, for example?

Here are some sections you might consider:

- Understairs cupboard
- Coat storage area
- Shoe storage area
- Console or hall tables
- Porch or vestibule

You may find your hallway is manageable in one session, but exercise that realism we keep harking back to and break it down into a project over a few days if necessary.

Physical Preparation and Logistics

You need to create an accessible sorting area before you begin, as often entryways are narrow and you might not be able to move around freely in them. The good news is there are always other rooms off a hallway, so your solution for where to sort items shouldn't be far away. Try and choose an area where you can spread items out, particularly if you have a large cupboard you are tackling as part of the project. If your sorting area can be in a room that's not in daily use (so you can work without interruption), even better.

Have bin bags ready for rubbish and recycling. Have a damp cloth and cleaning supplies to hand to wipe coat racks, baskets, shelving, boxes, radiators etc. And your vacuum cleaner will be helpful to get into all those nooks and crannies. If you're working in a cupboard and the light is compromised, make sure you have access to a torch.

As with all successful decluttering sessions, your exit plan is vital. Be sure you have an idea in mind of which of your decluttered items can go where and the time scheduled to make the necessary arrangements. If you have bulky items that you think you'll let go of, do you have space to store them before they leave your home?

Then, before you get started on the doing, make a record of where you are now by documenting it. Grab your phone and take a photo or video, so you can return to it later and see just how far you've come. Now you've taken stock, are you ready? We're going in!

The doing

How and Where to Get Started

The biggest part of this project is going to be any storage areas you have in your hallway because the amount of stuff that will be stored there will take your breath away. But storage cupboards in your entryway are incredibly useful, so we owe it to ourselves and our homes to make them work optimally. So, if you have an understairs cupboard, or any large storage cupboard, it's therefore best to begin by breaking the back of it first, even though it's going to take a while. It's time to tame the Tardis.

Ultimately, in your cupboards, you are aiming to have only those things that are serving you well in your current life, so decluttering will be key. But the real job here is to organise this cupboard in such a way that you can find the contents easily when you want them, and to ensure the items are easy to access, too. So, think visibility and accessibility all the way.

But these cupboards can be awkward. Sloping ceilings, overly deep shelves, shelves that are too high to reach without a step ladder. You need to factor these things in, find workarounds for awkward nooks and crannies, and create a space that becomes a cupboard of glee rather than a cupboard of gloom.

The key is to allow yourself space to navigate by using a separate sorting area, whether that's in your hallway or in an adjoining room.

Don't just dump the contents of the cupboard next to the cupboard door, for example, otherwise you'll be compromising your safety and the safety of your stuff. Before you begin, it's therefore important to think about how you are going to work in this area (which needs to be a thoroughfare) without compromising day-to-day life in your home.

To start work on your cupboard, pull things out and pre-sort them as you move them into the sorting area you have established, whether that be the dining table in the next room or on your living room floor. Gathering like with like at this stage will make it much easier to use the decluttering questions that follow, which will help you with your decision-making.

Once your larger storage areas are done you can move on to the smaller areas in your entryway: console tables, coat hooks, shoe bins. The volume of items in these places should be much smaller, so you may be able to declutter in situ rather than moving things into the sorting area you have established. The decluttering questions on p. 164 will help you assess what decisions to make about your things. Start with the bigger items you find, to make an immediate impact.

Decluttering Category by Category

It's a tough ask to try and come up with a list of what is typically in a hallway, but one thing's for sure, we need to accept the limitations of the space we have and make it work the very best it can for us.

As well as a hallway being a launch pad for daily activities, it can become a bulk-storage area too, for things like DIY equipment, suitcases, sentimental items and so on. Some of you will undoubtedly have items in your hallway that we have already discussed in the indoor and outdoor storage chapters, so we're going to focus here instead on the types of things we've not covered yet. (Although feel free to flip back to Chapter 7 and Chapter 8 if you need a reminder about any of the items already covered.) We've said it before and we'll say it again: no two homes are the same.

In an entryway, you'll typically find coats, shoes, umbrellas, hats, scarves and gloves. Then we have bags: school bags, handbags, sports bags, shopping bags, laptop bags, tote bags and plastic bags. We may even have suitcases and holdalls too.

Often, people need to house cleaning equipment in a hallway, so vacuum cleaners, brushes, mop buckets and all the paraphernalia that goes along with them can be found here. Maybe some of your most-used DIY equipment is kept in a hall cupboard too and, if you don't have any outside space, then paint, car stuff and perhaps wallpaper may be found in there too.

If you don't have a utility room, then step ladders, ironing boards and clothes airers often end up in hallway cupboards as the next best thing. If you have kids, then prams, car seats and rain covers can be huge space invaders in a hall. Pets need their own stuff too, so poo bags, leads, collars and coats are all often found near the front or back door.

On those 'handy' hallway surfaces, we find paperwork, takeaway leaflets, phone and address books and keys. And other bits and bobs, such as lightbulbs, batteries, bulbs and shoe cleaning equipment, and let's not forget visible reminders too (such as letters to be posted and other items to leave the house). These are thrown into the mix as well.

There's more – there's always more – but for now we have introduced only a fairly conservative list of what can be found in an entry space, and from this alone it's easy to see the problem. Our hallways need to work hard! So, it's time to pare down. Less is more when it comes to a hallway, so you definitely need to be strong when making your decluttering decisions.

We're going to go category by category and break it down as we dig into the emotions we chatted through earlier on p. 153. The following list of questions will help with this, as it'll allow us to determine which items you do actually use, challenge your previous decisions to keep certain items, and guide you towards items you can potentially live without and declutter.

Some of the items won't be applicable for you, some of the emotions won't resonate, but many of them will, so here we go.

COATS

- Do you have coats buried under other coats that you no longer wear or forgot you had?
- Are any coats too small or too big?
- Can you rehome some of the out-of-season coats or the ones you wear less frequently to a bedroom wardrobe?
- Are all the coats clean and ready to wear? Do you need to wash or dry-clean them?
- Have you emptied the pockets of all the coats?

BAGS

- Do you still use *all* the bags in the hallway, or do you favour newer ones with the older ones left gathering dust?
- If you have more shopping bags than you could carry or fit into a supermarket trolley, are you ever going to use them?
- If you have seldom-used handbags in the hallway, for example ones you would only use at a wedding, can you rehome them in another area?
- Do you have laptop bags you bought for an older model years ago that are too big and bulky for the computer you now use?
- Do you have book bags or sports bags for your kids that they have outgrown?
- Are all the bags emptied with regularity so that the contents from them are stored with similar items and not overlooked?
- If you have to store suitcases or holdalls in the entryway, is there scope to store smaller ones inside larger ones?

DIY EQUIPMENT

- Do you need to keep all your tools in the entryway, or could you just have a selection of your most-used things here so they're readily available? Do you have an obvious place to store the rest?
- Have you gone through your DIY stuff to ensure that all of it is realistic and useful?

- Is the paint you are keeping currently on a wall somewhere? How long has it been since you touched up paint? Is it actually never going to be used but you have kept it out of habit?

BABY AND TODDLER EQUIPMENT

- Is any of the stuff you are keeping no longer in use?
- Does the place where you keep your pram or car seat look intentional? Does it have a designated spot in your hallway to attempt to keep things as neat as possible?
- Can you keep some of this stuff in a bulk-storage area, such as a loft or basement, to free up space in this prime real estate of your home?

PET STUFF

- Have you decluttered your pet stuff recently to offload things that are surplus to requirement?
- Have you done an inventory of your pet stuff, so you don't buy duplicates?

PAPERWORK AND POST

- Do you have junk mail that can be recycled straightaway?
- If you have takeaway leaflets, do you look at the paper version or order online?

KEYS

- Do you know what every key is for?
- Have you tried all the keys and asked everyone whether they are required?

RANDOM BITS AND BOBS

- Are the bulbs you have all ones you can use?
- Are all the batteries in date?
- Is all that shoe cleaning equipment something you would use, or did you just fall foul of an upsell in a shop?

VISUAL REMINDERS

- Do you have visual reminders in the hallway that haven't been actioned yet? For example, dry-cleaning that hasn't been dropped off yet, library books that haven't been returned?

Storage Solutions

Let's remind ourselves of the overarching goal here. We are trying to create an area that lends itself to having everything we need to start the day visible and accessible to us, while also creating a space that feels warm and inviting when we return. So, in short, the hallway needs to work well on exit and entry. Be sure to keep on reminding yourself of your big-picture goals so you stay firmly on track.

Bear in mind that our homes, our lives and our families evolve constantly. A hallway that works for a retired couple and their day-to-day life is going to look very different to a hallway of a family with two toddlers in tow. What works for one doesn't necessarily work for the other and what worked before may not work now. The fact that you have removed a lot of the things from your hallway will allow you a fresh perspective. We become **clutter blind**, particularly in the high-traffic areas of our homes, so seeing a clear, uncluttered space will give clarity and guidance.

JARGON BUSTER

Clutter blind – the point at which we become so accustomed to seeing the things around us that we fail to identify it as a build-up of clutter.

Having decluttered means we'll have fewer things to store, so that's a win in itself. But, as we look at the storage and organisation in this space, there will undoubtedly be storage that we are currently using that works well and storage that doesn't.

For the storage that isn't working well, assess the barriers that are stopping it from operating effectively. Where are things piling up and looking unwieldy? What items are cumbersome to get to? What systems do we have that other people in the house aren't using properly? What would we really like to be different?

Once we have evaluated our current systems and storage, it's time to consider what changes, if any, we need to make. If you can introduce the right storage into your hallway, it can be a game-changer. Here are some things to consider:

Install more coat hooks. More hooks with fewer coats looks neater than fewer hooks with more coats, and this allows for greater visibility and accessibility too. Make sure your coat hooks are strong and fit for purpose. Fancy coat hooks look amazing with no coats on them, but the effect is lost when they're full! Installing lower hooks, if you have young kids, will allow them the opportunity to get into good habits and hang their own coats up.

Think about the throughput of shoes. Are all your shoes downstairs or do some stay upstairs? How many shoes are likely to be in your hallway on a standard day? Be sure to use or buy a container that will accommodate them all. Evaluate your needs carefully before you buy something that promises a great solution. Storage ideas in shops or online are rarely displayed with an abundance of stuff on them. Tap into the realism you are developing as part of this journey to ensure your decluttering success.

Avoid micro-organising. As well as creating an area that has the space to allow for your household's needs, be sure you create a system that everyone can use. If your kids aren't going to put shoes neatly into a shoe rack, will a box do? If a lidded box means everyone is putting their shoes on top rather than inside, maybe it's time to remove the lid. Then the shoes are stored together, the container looks intentional. It may not be how you envisaged things, but done is better than perfect.

Store hats, gloves and scarves out of the way. Can you store them higher up when out of season? You can try using vertical storage for this. For example, put a shelf above your coat hooks that is wide enough to house boxes or baskets for hats, gloves and scarves when they're not in regular use.

Introduce cubed storage. Cubed storage works really well in a hallway to house all the bits and bobs we need for our day-to-day lives, such as umbrellas, sports stuff, pet stuff and bags. It also allows for large volumes of items to be neatly stored until needed.

Have a designated home for your keys. If you are forever getting stalled trying to find important items when you're leaving the house, they need a spot. Somewhere non-negotiable for your keys, your work bag, the kids' PE kits, the dog's poo bags. Give them a home and you'll save so much time.

Use stackable boxes. If you're using an understairs cupboard then stackable boxes work really well. Make sure they are not too big or overly heavy (and make sure they are labelled). Create a system where the most-used items are easier to access. If you can create walking space, even better. Add wall hooks to maximise storage, and the more light there is the better. An understairs cupboard can seem like a game of *Tetris* but put in the time and it will pay dividends in the end.

Add extra shelves. If you have a hallway cupboard that is not awkward but has shelves that are too far apart, think about adding additional shelves horizontally to make the space more user-friendly. If your shelves are deep, find containers that reach all the way to the back and will allow you to slide them out as if they were drawers.

Use a visual map for large, deep cupboards. If you do have a large cupboard with numerous categories of items, create a map in the same way we did in our indoor and outdoor bulk-storage areas (on p. 125 and p. 150). That will help others find what they need.

Organising and Categorising

We're really getting there with the entryway project. By now, the sorting area will have lots of items you have decided to keep as they are useful or necessary in your current life. And importantly, with the space empty, you have taken a fresh look at the storage you have been using and made decisions on whether it needs an upgrade.

Assess the groups of items you have gathered together. Look at the volumes of things you have. Can you do a second pass at all to pare down even more?

When assessing your categories again, decide which items you use most frequently. In a hallway there are going to be things that are used seasonally, things that are used weekly and things that are used daily. Make sure the place where you decide to store your items represents the frequency of use. The most-used things should be easy to access, and lesser-used things can be in the trickier-to-get-to places. A hallway should allow priority access to those things that are going to facilitate the right start to your day and a simple system that will allow you easily to put the day away when you come in.

So now – you've guessed it – it's time to start putting things back category by category. It can sometimes be like trying to piece together a puzzle so don't be afraid to try different options until you find one that feels most sensible.

The Finishing Touches

Now you have decluttered and organised, you may have a collection of things that need to be actioned: library books to return, dry-cleaning to drop off, letters to post. Be sure to make a conscious effort to finish the job by actioning these outstanding tasks. You'll need to remove any decluttered items from the home and grab your vacuum cleaner to clean those pictures and lights that are up high.

Oh, and now, at long last, it's time to bring in form. Once you have a functional working space, you can add the finishing touches, such as photos, ornaments, pictures and candles, so that when you come through the door it feels like a home you can be proud of and want to be in.

Take a new 'after' photo or video so you can remind yourself of the progress you have made. And prepare yourself for everyone else in your home to ignore your perfect space next time they walk through the door! (Only this time, you'll be ready and waiting with a place for everything, so you can put everything back in its place. Result!) Honestly, getting the entryways to your home right is a game-changer. It will help your household to operate more efficiently and make or break your day or evening.

Take stock of the calm that you will undoubtedly feel now that you have done such vital and impactful work on your hallway. We hope you feel in control and are happy that the choices you have made are the right ones for you and those around you. As your decluttering muscle is well and truly flexed and ready for more now, take a quick breather and then it's time to move into those areas of your home you probably wanted to do aeons ago.

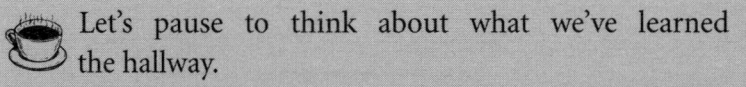

TAKE A MOMENT

Let's pause to think about what we've learned in the hallway.

- Are the foundations you are building upon affecting your desire to make more progress? How?
- Will you commit more to daily resets now you have established storage solutions and ideas that are more functional? How?
- Is a decluttered, organised hallway affecting your relationship with your home? How?

10

Books

'When does a collection become clutter?'

The mere mention of the word 'books' in a decluttering context has people running for the hills. Books are inspiring, helpful, educational, entertaining and so many things in between. Something we share. Something we covet. Something we enjoy. But more than that, books are something that we don't want to offer up in the decluttering arena, even though we know it's long overdue. We've been there so many times with clients and members who urge us to step away from the books. Every other area of the home is fair game, but books are off-limits.

We purposely left books until much later in our decluttering journey so that our decluttering muscle would be stronger, and now it's time to take action. Convincing a book lover to even try to evaluate their book collection is one of the biggest challenges we face as professional organisers, but we're going to give it our best shot. We urge you not to skip past this chapter as the time to take action is now.

How many books you have is a very personal choice. But the significant factor that will dictate how many books you *should* have in your home is the space you have to store them. If there are rooms in your home that have become overwhelmed with books, it's time to create some order and identify which books are less deserving of their spot than others.

We are going to look at the psychology of why we love and own books first, including why some people are drawn to them in large volumes, while others are happy to keep very few. Then we're going to look at the logic and accessibility of your book storage system, and the compromises we may need to make in order for it to work optimally. If we choose to keep books in the home, we need to ensure we have a system that means we can find what we need, when we need it and, of course, that our particularly precious books are protected and maintained.

Now, you may be wondering what on earth we're talking about. Maybe you're someone who is able to buy a book, read it and pass it on without a second thought. You may have curtailed your overabundance of books years ago by moving to audiobooks or e-books. If books are not your thing then feel free to gloss over this chapter and move into your next target area, which begins on p. 189.

But for everyone else, it's time to embrace an open mind and a fresh perspective. Are you ready for a journey into the world of collections?

The thinking

Emotional Preparation

COLLECTION VERSUS CLUTTER

The single biggest issue that holds people back from tackling their books is thinking of their books as a collection. If we view a category of items as a collection, whether it is books or not, this presents an immediate barrier that stops us from making headway with our clutter problem, because the decision to split that collection is tortuous.

So, we need to first understand that books are individual items, each of which must vie for their position in our homes. Without making this mental leap towards breaking down our collections, we will struggle to make progress.

What's interesting about books, though, compared to any other item we've discussed and decluttered so far, is that more often than not, books have a designated home already. Books are usually stored on a bookcase, neatly stacked like with like, maybe even categorised and zoned. Because books commonly hold a special place in our hearts, we have often given time and attention over the years to organise them in this way. As a result, we do not see books as being as wayward as other categories of stuff in our homes. For this reason, we often decide that a book collection is not bothering anyone, so it goes down the pecking order of decluttering projects.

If you are a book lover (and favour a physical book over a digital version), you will undoubtedly acquire more as you move through life. Let me paint you a scenario. As your book collection has grown, so too has the volume and, out of nowhere, your books may suddenly appear everywhere: on a bookshelf here, double stacked there, piled on the floor, even under the bed… Everywhere you look there's a book or a pile of books, or so it seems. To avoid this it's therefore vital that you establish a process that facilitates a regular throughput of less-desirable books to make space for new ones.

The collection therefore needs to be broken down to evaluate it item by item. You need to ensure that every single book in your home adds value to your current life. Let's face it, a novelty joke book we got from a colleague as a Secret Santa gift or a chick flick we picked up at the airport is not the same as a treasured book we were given by a grandparent for our 21st birthday. Our job is to split our collection down and evaluate each book we own to establish where it sits on the desirability scale.

NOSTALGIC NUANCE

Books can feel like an intrinsic part of you. Some books are foundational. That travel guide that accompanied you from Milan to Morocco in your twenties. That Jamie Oliver book you always rely on for your Yorkshire pudding recipe. Some books are nostalgic, too, for example the Harry Potter series that saw you grow from child to adult. The pop-up book you read with your children over and over that's falling apart now because it was always the one they selected from the bookshelf each night. We could go on, but you understand. There are books in life that are gems that will always warrant their spot because they feel like a part of us.

But there are so many more that need to be scrutinised. Do we need to keep *all* the books we read with our children when they were small? Are there some self-help books we abandoned after 30 laborious pages, like the 'I can make you thin' book that just didn't deliver. That long line of recipe books at the back of the shelf with pages as clean as the day they were bought (apart from the dust on top). Those encyclopaedias we received as a child that we've seen but never looked at in over 20 years. These are the types of books whose value we need to question.

All these books form a part of our past for sure, but one book is not the same as the other. Our bookshelves should not be so full of nostalgia and sentiment that there is no space for the ones that are interesting to us right here, right now. As our lives evolve, so too do our book choices. A book decluttering project is all about finding the quality and ditching the quantity.

INSPIRATION OR ASPIRATION

It's time to tap into realism again and work out which books we are keeping because they are aspirational. Are we buying books because we think we 'ought' to read them – think along the lines of *Jane Eyre* and *Great Expectations*? Are we displaying books that we think will make us appear well-read? That coffee table design book that looks impressive, but you've never opened.

Are we keeping hold of self-help books in the hope that the issue we have will fix itself by osmosis? Self-help books are there to inspire and facilitate action. Popping them on a shelf and hoping for a transformation is not going to get the job done. The irony is not lost on us that this is a decluttering book and indeed falls into the self-help category, but if this book isn't serving its purpose and giving you actionable steps that you can take to alleviate your decluttering problem, please do yourself a favour and add it to your next donation pile. Our hope is that this will become the foundational self-help book that you will revisit again and again as needed, but only you will know.

Our bookshelves are often packed to the brim with books that are waiting around for us to suddenly decide that today's the day, but today never comes. Life's too short for reading things that are laborious and unhelpful. Seek out inspiration rather than aspiration. Let go of the book, let go of the guilt.

To Sell or Not to Sell

Google estimates that there are 129 million unique books in the world. That's a lot of books. And with over 2 million new titles being added every year is it any wonder we are becoming overrun? But with so many printed books already in circulation, coupled with the move to digital, our opportunity to pass books on to new homes is becoming more limited. Charity shops are becoming selective about what they will accept and selling books delivers pennies in return.

The trade in second-hand books is undoubtedly a buyers' market. You can spend time listing books on apps and selling sites but is it worth your while? Are we overestimating the value of books because they form part of a category of items that we feel very attached to? Are we spending 30 minutes of our precious time photographing, listing and posting a book for a 99p gain? There are, of course, exceptions that prove the rule. Some books, such as first editions or rare books, have real value. A quick search on a bookselling site will give you an indication of whether investing time and energy into recouping money by selling is the best use of your precious time.

We advise you to reframe your thinking and make decluttering, not selling, your primary goal. After all, that's the reason you're here. Donation is a simple option, so we suggest you accept that the money's gone and pass the item on.

Location, Location, Location

If you're embarking on a project to declutter and organise your books, it is important you spend time working out the right place for them in your home. Does their current location make sense? Do you have books from the same categories in several locations? How much space are you willing to, and is sensible to, dedicate to book storage?

Books can be stored in so many different places. But where are they in your home? The list is endless. If you are a book lover, the chances are you have installed a bookcase almost everywhere where there is space for one. Books are in the living room, on shelves in the kitchen, on bedside tables, in children's bedrooms, in spare bedrooms, in home offices, on landings and in hallways too, with often an overflow in boxes in the attic or garage.

THE WRONG LOCATION FOR BOOKS

As part of your decluttering, try to make sure you haven't got any books in your indoor or outdoor storage areas (as discussed in Chapters 7 and 8). This can cause problems because garages and sheds can be very damp, which will ruin your books. Also, heavy boxes of books can be a real strain on loft rafters. It is also tricky and dangerous to manoeuvre books up and down a loft ladder.

But the most important thing to consider about storing books in lofts, garages, sheds and storage units (or your poor parents' homes) is that once it's gone into a box, it will probably never see the light of day again. The old adage 'out of sight, out of mind' has never been truer. If you have such a surplus of books that your only option is for them to be in boxes, we advise it's time to declutter some and bid them farewell.

THE RIGHT LOCATION FOR BOOKS

Think logically about where the sensible place to house your books would be. This will, of course, be different depending on the layout of your home, who lives in your household with you, and the volumes and categories of books you have, but here's a basic starting point:

Cookbooks should be stored in the kitchen if there is ample space or, as an alternative, in the living room or dining room if that is where you explore recipes and do your meal planning.

Children's books should either be in their bedroom or where they play.

Academic and work-related books should be stored in a home office, close to your desk or near to where you work on your laptop or computer, especially if you use your books for regular reference.

Books read for pleasure should be kept as close as possible to where you read. This is, of course, likely to be at least two places: your living area and your bedroom.

If you are lucky enough to have a room set up as a library or with ample bookcases, you will have the luxury of categorising everything so it will be much easier to search for a book when needed.

Bear in mind that if a book isn't stored in the room where you generally use it, it creates a barrier to putting it back. Books then start to pile up and the clutter starts to build.

TAKE A MOMENT

Do any of the habits and emotions we've mentioned strike a chord? It's important to take a realistic look at our own habits to determine how we are going to work through this area of our homes.

- Have you struggled to break down your collection?
- Are your shelves so overwhelmed with nostalgia and sentiment that there's no space for new books?
- Are you guilty of keeping books because you feel like you ought to read them?
- Do you struggle to let go because you can't recoup the value you perceive the books have?
- Do you have books in boxes in your bulk-storage areas?

Goal Setting

BIG-PICTURE GOALS

Books are no exception when it comes to creating a big-picture goal that is going to keep you focused and motivated. Below are some potential big-picture goals that may resonate with you. You may have one goal or you may have several, and that's fine.

Curate your collection

Your big-picture goal may be to develop a system in your book collection. If your high school dictionary is squashed in next to your thrillers, and your gardening books are sitting next to your autobiographies, maybe it's time to create some order. Would you love to have your books displayed by genre so you can more easily find what you need? Having a curated, well-ordered, categorised inventory is so satisfying and offers the best opportunity for you to truly make the most of the investment you have made in your books.

Reconnection

Whether you have a manageable quantity of books or a larger volume, one of the most satisfying outcomes of a book declutter is the opportunity to reconnect with your books. This is important because, as books are often on a shelf or bookcase, it means we aren't constantly noticing them. Consequently, we get to a stage where we stop seeing what we have; we see only the collection rather than the individual components. Evaluating each book one by one creates the opportunity to reconnect with books we have not seen in a while. And that simple reconnection gives us the opportunity to create an inventory to facilitate doing with them what life intended: reading. This is a very rewarding and very relevant big-picture goal.

Shop from home

If you can't walk past your local bookshop without succumbing to the latest releases, you eagerly snap up all the Book Club recommendations or regularly scour the charity shop for new purchases, maybe your big-picture goal could be to start 'shopping from home'. You could finally work through the hundreds of books from your last spree, currently unread. The nice thing about this goal is that it will also allow for longer-term progress with your decluttering, as every time you finish a book it allows a further opportunity for letting go.

Don't double up

If your volumes are large, you may have got to a stage where your bookcases or shelves are double stacked. While this offers a solution from a storage perspective, it prevents accessibility and visibility and should be avoided. Your big-picture goal therefore may be to eliminate any double stacking of books. This will require bold decision-making and may take several phases to achieve, as it will probably mean decluttering a significant number of books, but the outcome is so worth it.

Banish the boxes

And now we come to a big-picture goal that, for us, is non-negotiable. In the same way that eliminating double stacking allows all your books to be seen, so too does taking books out of boxes. Books in a garage, loft, attic or basement are out of sight, out of mind. Books ought to be given at least a fighting chance of being read and if they are in a box, unseen, untouched and unloved, this is never going to happen. Unless a transitional period is taking place in your life, such as a renovation or house move, books belong in the body of the home, and you should try your utmost to achieve this.

Think about what is going to motivate you, write it down and let's prepare ourselves for the project.

Planning Section by Section

Now you've thought carefully about the task ahead it's time to look at how your book project is going to unfold. We need to find a sensible route through all the books in our homes – breaking them down into sections – so that we can make the project more achievable and sensible.

Does it make sense to work category by category, shelf by shelf or bookcase by bookcase? The volume of books you have is going to dictate how much you need to break this project down, so do some evaluation first. For example, if you have hundreds of children's books, gather them together first and do that category separately before moving on to the next category. (Suggestions of how to work category by category are in the categorisation section that follows, on p. 185.)

Physical Preparation and Logistics

Before we get started, a reminder that a book declutter can be tough physically because books are heavy items and are often scattered around the house. Therefore, if one of your goals is to store your books together, you may have some heavy lifting to undertake, so be sure you have help at hand if needed to bring those boxes down from the attic or up from the basement.

If you want to relocate books from elsewhere inside the home, you are going to need something to carry them in, so grab a box or large bag to transport them more easily.

Fetch some cleaning supplies because sorting through your books can get dusty. You will be emptying shelves and bookcases that have not been touched in possibly years, so do remember during the project to move furniture and vacuum behind what you can.

Logistically, you are going to need space to sort, so identify a flat surface you can work on. This could be the floor if you feel able to move freely or a large table or sofa where you can sort things into piles. Plan to do your sorting as close as possible to where your books are stored to avoid unnecessary moving and carrying back and forth.

Once you commit to a book declutter, the amount of items you are letting go can be huge, so you need to be ready for what's coming. Grab some heavier-grade bin bags or small boxes to help you with your decluttered books. Thin bin bags split easily when they come into contact with the weight or corners of books, and there's nothing more annoying than having to rescue books that have broken free, so grab some bin bags that are robust.

The chances are you will work out an exit plan for your books that involves more than one destination, maybe a charity shop, a friend, a giveaway site, a selling app or a return to the local library. Knowing that you are passing an unwanted book to someone who will enjoy it can be a brilliant incentive. The books can enjoy a second life. If you have a beneficiary in mind, check in advance that they want your unwanted books and that this is not just your way of passing on your clutter to someone else who has the same issue with book clutter as you.

So, we've done the thinking and it's time for action. Let the book decluttering commence!

The doing

How and Where to Get Started

There's no doubt that decluttering books can be an overwhelming task, so where is the best place to start? There isn't a straightforward answer to this really because there are so many different scenarios in people's homes. You may have books spread out across several rooms and want to retain that system. You may have books predominantly in one room but have had to create little pockets of overflow dotted around. You may have books stored in boxes that you want to incorporate into your main book storage area. So, how do you tackle it?

We advise you get started in your main book storage area. That way you can make inroads there and create space with a view to bringing in books further down the line from other overflow areas, based on the big-picture goals we talked about on p. 178.

You can start by taking books off your bookshelves and separating them into different categories. (We'll talk through these different categories on p. 185.) When it comes to books, more often than not, there is already an element of categorisation in place (as we mentioned at the beginning of this chapter) even if the categories have become a little wayward over the years. You may have all your novels together, all your cookery books together, or all your reference books together, for example. If that's the case, it makes sense to try to retain the categorisation that has already been established.

Sometimes other people's books form part of what we will be looking at, so how do we deal with that? We strongly advise you not to declutter the books of another family member without their consent. This is, in fact, our advice about all items in the home. Create a pile of their books, categorise them and they can then look through and decide which ones are going or staying at a later stage. If they have no intention of being involved in the main decluttering process, breaking it down into small, manageable categories for them is the key.

If you're going through young children's books you can make decisions, but if they are older, they can either help you or you can create a stack of books you think can go, but we suggest you then allow them to have the final say on each item. It's useful to tackle other people's books as a separate project so you don't get waylaid.

Start sorting the things you are letting go into piles and, if possible, put them into labelled bags or boxes straight away. Always be sure not to overload book bags as they are heavy and cumbersome.

Have a good look at your books before donating them. If they are torn, scribbled in or dirty, send them for recycling instead. Sometimes, due to the glue in the book binding, some recycling centres won't recycle them with the other paper products so please check locally. Make sure you give the books that are being donated, returned or gifted a flick through to see if there are any bookmarks, postcards, tickets or even money in them. You don't want that £20 gift card finding its way to the local charity shop!

Decluttering Questions

When you are looking at whether or not something deserves its place in your home, it's fair to say that answering some simple questions can help you make a decision on the lion's share of your books. So, take one book at a time, hold it in your hand and evaluate the questions below:

- Do you have more than one copy?
- Is it musty, falling apart or does it have pages sticking together?
- Is it a novel you have read and wouldn't read again?
- Is it a book you started and disliked?
- Is it a medical/business/academic book that contains outdated theories or practices?
- Is it a novelty book?
- Would someone you know enjoy this book more than you?
- Do you have an e-book or audiobook version, or could you easily get hold of one?

If the answer to any of these questions is yes, then the item is definitely a serious contender to let go of. And, if you are letting it go, put it straight into the correct bin bag based on your exit plan.

As we've mentioned, decluttering books can be tough emotionally and your first instinct may be to keep most of them. However, if you are inundated with books and have made a decision to try and be braver in your decision-making, you may need to dig deeper. Often, it is only when you actually get started with decluttering that you realise just how deep-seated some of the emotions are.

But remember, small wins mean large gains when it comes to books. Ten or 15 books decluttered can mean freeing up a whole shelf. So, commit to that first mental leap, enjoy reconnecting with books you had forgotten about, resist the urge to start reading the books you stumble across, and get started!

Dig deeper

If you've started decluttering and made some sensible decisions, but still feel as if you have too many for your space, we might need to go deeper. Here are some more probing questions you can ask yourself about your relationship with books:

- Do you keep books because you think you ought to read them to demonstrate your worth?
- Do you keep books because they look good to guests?
- Do you believe your book collection represents your sense of self and therefore you struggle to dismantle it?
- Do you hold on to self-help books in the hope that they may fix an issue you have?
- Do you keep hold of too many books for sentimental reasons?
- Are you holding on to books that your children have outgrown because you don't want to let go of their childhood?
- Are you holding on to books that you think will serve you in a future life?
- Are you keeping a book because you think it has commercial value?
- Are you keeping hold of a book because it is a signed copy?

These questions will get you thinking, but ultimately it all boils down to what is more important to you: the space or the stuff. But do remember, there is no right or wrong decision. These are your things, and it will always be your choice. The goal is to feel that you have made the right decision for the here and now. You can always return to your books in the future for the next phase.

Remember, it's vital at this stage to feel in control of not only your decluttering decisions but also the categorisation you are creating so that you don't make things difficult for yourself later. If it makes sense, divide the books you are keeping into broad categories such as children's books, novels, reference books and so on. It may be useful to create a 'want to read' category so you can store those on their own in a separate area to help with overbuying and facilitate shopping from home. Your categories will be fine-tuned later though; for now you are firmly in decluttering mode, so don't overthink categorisation at this point.

Cleaning

If you have a bookcase you can move, this is the time to pull it away from the wall and clean and vacuum behind it. It might be years before the opportunity arises again. You will also need to clean and wipe the shelves before returning any books.

Books can get very dusty over time so you might want to give them a wipe with a very lightly damp cloth, vacuum the top of the book or open the book in half and give it a gentle whack so the dust is dislodged. Do this by an open window to keep the dust at bay. If your books are very old and antique, you might want to use an unused paint brush to gently brush the dust off the book.

If you are buying new bookcases, consider ones with glass doors to keep the dust at bay. It makes cleaning and maintenance so much easier and will make sure your books stay in better condition for longer.

Organisation and Storage

CATEGORISATION

You've gone through your books and you've decided what you want to keep and what can go. You have assigned a loose categorisation to the books you have decided to keep, but now it's time to do some fine-tuning. Let's put your treasured books back and organise them well so you can find what you need easily. The main categories include:

- Travel guides
- Novels
- A–Zs
- Cookery
- Children's
- Atlases
- Encyclopaedias
- Music
- Academic

- Classics
- Autobiographies and biographies
- Self-help
- History
- Political
- Funny
- Poetry
- Home and interior design
- Medical and health

You may have some of the categories, you may have all of them, and you may have ones we haven't listed. Categorising books at this stage also gives us a second opportunity to revisit our favourites and really question whether a book is still useful or desirable. Once we categorise, it is easy to see duplicates, too.

Positioning

Before you start putting them all back on their shelves, think about their old location. Do you want your books to go back to where they were or do you need to move them to another, more suitable location? Do you have more or less of a certain category of book than you had anticipated? Take stock of your volumes and whether your initial idea of how much space you would need to allocate for each category still holds true.

If your books are staying on the shelves they were originally on, look at the spacing between the shelves and put larger books where you have more height and smaller books in the smaller shelves. If your shelves are adjustable, take the opportunity to maximise storage by adjusting them to fit your collection.

Put the same-height books together if they are in the same category. Putting books in height order makes a shelf look much more uniform and orderly. Sometimes it's not possible but you will almost certainly be able to do this on many of your shelves.

If you haven't got the space to give each category its own shelf, put similar categories together. Maybe your health books can go with cookbooks or self-help. Your poetry could go with classics or humorous books. Your atlases and A–Zs could go with travel books. Your classics could go with modern fiction, and so on. Work out a system that seems logical for you.

Also think about safety when deciding where books should be stored in a bookcase. Large and heavy books are better at the bottom of a bookcase, so you don't need to lift them down from high shelves and to prevent bookcases from becoming top-heavy and more likely to topple.

The one thing we wouldn't recommend is doubling up on bookshelves, i.e. putting one row of books in front of another row. It makes the books difficult to see and access, and means you are unlikely to use them. If you find yourself having to double up on books, further decluttering is suggested to pare down the volumes and leave you with a manageable, sensible amount that you can see and access easily.

The Finishing Touches

If you are a true book lover, completing this project will bring great joy. You will feel as if you have really turned a corner in an area of your home you feel very connected to. Removing books from your home creates a lot of space, so hopefully you will have been able to achieve all of your big-picture goals.

Sorting books is a project we leave until later in our decluttering journey because it can really test our emotions. But once you make that mental leap and allow yourself the opportunity to view each component as a single item, it propels you forwards into making a real, sustainable mindset change.

There are very few finishing touches to be done when it comes to books as we have done all the hard work. But your exit plan is waiting for you. Be sure to take your donations to the charity shop or pass them on to friends and family and, most of all, enjoy the special feeling of giving your coveted books that second life they deserve.

TAKE A MOMENT

 Let's take a moment to reflect on a job well done and think about the progress we are making:

- Have you been able to move out of your comfort zone more than you expected?
- Have you made any decisions about how you will ensure you are focusing on reading the books you have rather than acquiring new ones?
- Have you identified how you feel about having done this project at this point in your decluttering journey?
- Have you identified how you think delving into an area that can be tricky emotionally has helped you with your decluttering mindset?

11

The living room

'A place for everything and everything in its place.'

It's fair to say some living rooms have to work harder than others. In an ideal scenario, a living room would have comfy seating, a side table on which to pop a cup of tea or evening tipple, a few carefully curated ornaments, art and sentimental belongings, a TV (optional) and not much else.

But, for most of us, the reality of life, homes, people and stuff is quite different. The living room (most likely singular) needs to facilitate a whole myriad of work, rest and play tasks.

Our kids play in here, we craft in here, work in here, eat in here, scroll in here, think in here, read in here, watch TV in here – do we need to go on? The term multifunctional doesn't even do it justice. Let's add into the complex mix of uses we've already mentioned the fact that this room is likely to be where guests are welcomed into our homes. Here is where visitors cross the invisible border and get a window on our world, which we may not be ready for or comfortable with.

You see, every living room in every home looks completely different. What's stored here is going to be dictated not only by the configuration of your home but your family make-up, your hobbies, your memories, your habits and, of course, your emotional connection to things.

We're going to cover the most common categories of items you would find in a living room, one by one. Some of the things we mention may be elsewhere in your home. Some things you may have already tackled in earlier rooms of the home. If so, this will give you an opportunity to revisit those items, and the emotions relating to them, to ensure you have made the very best decisions you can.

And there may be things you have in your living room that we don't mention here. We can't cover every possible item and every scenario, but this is why we've held off talking about your living room until this later point in your decluttering journey: we feel confident that you are far enough along now to have learned the skills to tackle almost anything. (And that's what you need when decluttering the living room!)

We say *almost* anything because there is one omission. Sentimental items will undoubtedly be dotted around your living room. Once again, put them to one side, because we're going to tackle those in Chapter 12. Don't be tempted to jump ahead. Let's tackle the main components of the living area first and then give ourselves the time and space to enjoy the reconnection and curation components of decluttering our sentimental items in the next chapter.

A living room can be trickier than you think, but you've got this. It's time to have a room you want to be in and that you can feel proud of. You deserve it!

The thinking

Emotional Preparation

CLUTTER BLINDNESS

By this point, the practice of taking a photograph so that you can remind yourself of the fantastic progress you have made is probably firmly cemented in your mind. But we are now going to use photographs and videos for an entirely different purpose. This is because we need to make use of a brand-new set of eyes.

Over time, we become so accustomed to seeing the same things in the same rooms at the same time of day that we become what is known as clutter blind. All those little piles of magazines and the paperwork stuffed down the side of sofa; the paintings your child brought home six months ago curled up and dusty on your mantelpiece; all those DVDs that won't fit in the cabinet and are in little piles in front it instead – they are so familiar to us that we no longer see them with an evaluative eye.

So, let's take the time to snap a set of photos or a video to view the room through a different lens. If possible, look at the photo you have taken on a larger screen than your phone, to really enhance your view and gain the maximum impact. Trying to incite a fresh perspective on something can really help everywhere in your home, but the concept of clutter blindness is definitely at play in a living room because when we are in here we are almost always in 'relaxing mode' (as opposed to in the kitchen or bathroom where we are in 'doing mode'), so we are often not paying as much attention.

Now you have your new lens, can you more easily see those clutter heaps and hotspots? Can you identify areas of your room that detract from the calmness you'd like to feel? This process can be powerful when on a decluttering journey, so give it a try and you will get a better feel for what you're going to be working on. (And have the photo in your back pocket as a tool to pull out whenever it's time to revisit your decluttering in the future.)

FUNCTIONAL FURNITURE

Now we are firmly in evaluation mode, let's continue and look at the furniture we have. If you have lived with an excess of stuff in your home for years, the chances are that at some point you made a decision that the answer to your clutter problems was to acquire more storage. That may have been either bigger furniture or more containers. Trust us, you are not alone! Most of the homes we work in have storage galore – more often than not, way too much storage –

and that storage, whether it be a box, a shelf or a cupboard, becomes clutter too.

As you look around your room, does it feel overfull, not just with stuff but with furniture too? How is your storage looking? Is it a mishmash of all different textures, colours and sizes? Having storage that blends into the decor really makes a difference when working in a living room. Is your furniture oversize when it doesn't need to be? Do we have more chairs or side tables than we could ever sensibly use?

When people are trying to sell a home, one of the changes that has the most impact on a potential buyer's first impression is having less furniture. Think about show homes, think about magazine articles, think about TV makeover shows – the one thing they all have in common is that there is very little furniture, and the furniture that is in use is clever. It's all designed to store your things in a way that doesn't detract from a sense of calm and relaxation.

Do we not owe it to ourselves to have a room that exudes calm? When we look at the furniture we have, our task is to find the right balance of something that is both aesthetically pleasing but functional. We talked about form and function back on p. 155, so pop back to remind yourself of the key learnings if helpful. We need sufficient storage to house the things that we love, need or use around us in the right places, but we also need to ensure we don't have too much furniture that will detract from the ambience we are trying to create.

GUEST GOALS

When we talk to people about their desired outcome from decluttering, one of the most prevalent is the hope that one day people will be able to pop into your home unannounced without you experiencing an intense and overwhelming sense of panic.

Human interaction is such a vital component of our well-being, and the ability to have people over is important. Whether that's family popping in for a long-overdue catch-up; our children's friends coming over for a playdate; or professionals to help us resolve an issue. A living room is an obvious destination to invite guests into, so we will naturally want this room to feel welcoming.

If we are nervous about people entering our homes, we won't be putting our best foot forwards and that will impact the success of that interaction. If a friend has popped in, we want to ensure that they are not focused on our stuff rather than our conversation. If an expert is here to help, we don't want the state of our homes to be a talking point during their feedback to colleagues. (This takes us back to the judgement we talked about on p. 153, which is worth revisiting.)

While having guest goals is important, we'd like to reiterate that the most important person who should benefit from a decluttering journey is you, followed closely by the other people in your household. Guests are definitely further down the pecking order. Getting to the point where you welcome them into your home fearlessly with open arms might take a while, but it's always a nice little goal to have in your line of sight.

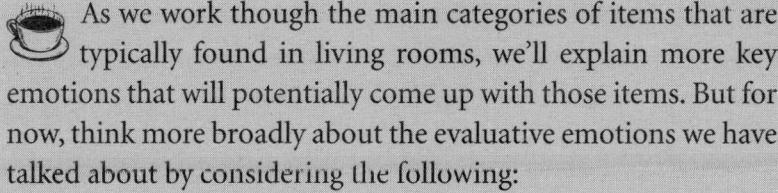

TAKE A MOMENT

As we work though the main categories of items that are typically found in living rooms, we'll explain more key emotions that will potentially come up with those items. But for now, think more broadly about the evaluative emotions we have talked about by considering the following:

- Have you become clutter blind to the things on your windowsill, on your mantelpiece or piled up on your coffee table?
- Have you bought furniture in the past to store your clutter? As your clutter mindset is changing, do you feel committed to letting go of some of the storage boxes and maybe even furniture?
- Have you found yourself slowly but surely going out to see friends rather than feeling comfortable about inviting them into your home?

Goal Setting

BIG-PICTURE GOALS

Before we get started, it's time to think of the big picture. Setting a big-picture goal for your living room will drive your motivation and keep you focused. Let's give you some examples of big-picture goals that may resonate with you for a living room:

Renovation-based goal. Maybe an overhaul of your living room is long overdue. Clearing the clutter makes a renovation possible. In fact, a room renovation is often the first thing people look at when the clutter in their home is gone.

Work- or study-based goal. Perhaps you need to create a computer area either for yourself or for someone else in your household. A new requirement to incorporate a computer into a living room requires a shift in thinking and a rejig of the room.

Hobby-based goal. You have a new hobby that has items associated with it. You need to find a suitable spot to carry out your hobby and tidy the things away after use. Decluttering is all about making space for the things you *do* want in your life, so this is an important one.

Transition-based goal. There's a change in circumstance and your room needs to reflect that. It could be a new baby, recuperation from an illness, two households becoming one, the loss of a partner. All these transitions mean changes may be needed in your living room.

Guest-based goal. You would just like people to come into your home without judging you. Honestly, this is one of the biggest wins when it comes to decluttering. Judgement weighs heavily on us and sometimes it's only when that has been eradicated you see just how much of a burden it was.

Of course, your goal may be several or all of the above. You may just want to create a multi-purpose room that works equally well for all the things life throws at it. Spend some time thinking about what big-picture goal is driving you towards success in your living room now and jot it down to keep it front of mind.

Planning Section by Section

The most important thing to consider when you are preparing to embark on decluttering your living room is to work out what categories of item you might have to tackle, and how you will be able to break it down. Doing this project in small, manageable chunks is more important than ever because, at some point soon, you or your family are going to want to come in here to do what you need to do, so we need to be very mindful to avoid the **messy middle**.

JARGON BUSTER

Messy middle – the period during a decluttering project where you have taken lots of things out but not yet started to put things away. Consequently, it feels messy, overwhelming and as if it will never be completed.

We will potentially come across what will feel like very random categories of items in the living room. They need to be given the attention they deserve (more about that in the doing section on the next page). Even though these categories are narrow and often contain few items, and are often difficult to work with, we mustn't rush as we want to do the living room thoroughly and make rational decisions about what stays and goes. The success of the living room project is going to be based on the care and attention we give it and the focus we apply to finding storage solutions that will work.

Refer to the decluttering section on p. 197 to determine how to break this project down.

Physical Preparation and Logistics

You need to consider where you can sort your items. Do you have boxes or crates you can use to stack things up if you are in the middle of your project and have to finish for the day? This will help you feel in control regardless of how many sessions this project spans. And we suggest having some bigger sticky labels or postcards so you can keep track of where you are by labelling information on to each box.

As always, you need to think about an exit plan. Since there are lots of different types of items in this room you may need to recycle, rehome or return different things to different parts of the home. These are all going to require different exit plans, so do your planning and identify your outlets before you get started. Different-coloured bin bags are helpful so you can keep control of what's going where.

Grab those cleaning supplies so you can clean as you go and, if you can clean behind furniture, now's the time to do it. A label maker is going to be helpful here too, so, if you have one, make sure it has batteries and tape.

It's time to take your 'before' photo, then we're ready to go in!

The doing

How and Where to Get Started

Have a cursory glance around the room to determine whether any of the items you have been historically storing in here can now be moved into other areas of your home that you have already tackled and created space in. You will still need to go through the decluttering process for any items you rehome from the living space, but this is best done in the room that will be the item's final destination. Do you have things in here that can now be moved into your freshly decluttered kitchen or garage, for example your cookery books or toys that are going to be rotated?

The number of categories and the volumes of stuff you have in your living room are going to dictate how you should tackle this project. But, as far as is practical, try to tackle each category that we talk through below one at a time.

This methodical approach is important for two reasons. First, taking one category at a time will help you feel a gradual sense of accomplishment as you work through this project. Second, working in this ordered way will ensure you're not dragging everything out of each and every storage space you have, which would make it challenging for you or the other members of your household when they inevitably want to use the room to relax in later today.

If necessary, use a checklist to keep track of what's been done and what's still to come. It all helps to keep your motivation boosted in what can be a very disjointed room. Let's begin.

Decluttering Category by Category

Some of the categories listed below may not be in your living area. If they are elsewhere in your home instead (and if you haven't tackled them yet), remember to come back to them later, wherever they are situated in your home.

MAGAZINES AND NEWSPAPERS

Before you get started with newspapers and magazines, ascertain how much of a problem this category is for you. Do you just have a build-up from the past couple of weeks to sort or have you been getting multiple magazines on subscriptions for years that are still in their wrappers unopened and unread?

If you are in the former camp, this will be a quick fix. Just look through what you have and make a value judgement as to whether you will actually find the time or inclination to read these magazines. If not, pop them straight into recycling and don't look back.

If you are in the latter category, you are going to need to take your time. If you have been an object gatherer over the years, chances are you are an information gatherer too. Let's get serious. How likely is it you will refer back to instructions from a November 2015 article on how to ice the perfect Christmas cake? When you last booked a holiday, did you go rifling through your stacks of travel mags to find that hotel that caught your eye three years ago? And how many patterns do you already have still waiting in your 'ideas' pile?

We need to tap into the realism we now understand so well and recognise the aspirational barrier rearing its head again. Ask yourself these questions:

- Do you habitually buy a magazine as part of your weekly trip to the supermarket without giving it a second thought?
- Does your monthly subscription just pop through the letterbox only to be added to the unread pile with the others?
- Do you feel guilty about the money you feel you have wasted on magazines and newspapers in the past, which means you have been keeping hold of way too many for too long now?

When you are making a decision to declutter and organise magazines and newspapers, you may need a phased approach. If you have been a committed information gatherer, it's not that easy to go from all to nothing overnight. Think of a timescale for keeping your magazines or newspapers that is significantly less than the length of time you'd normally keep them for. For example, if you have historically kept magazines for five years or more, could you think about just keeping the ones from this year? Ensure your new time-based goal seems sensible and achievable and stick to it. Keep the ones that fulfil that criteria and let go of the rest.

DINING SETS

You may be wondering why dining sets are in the living room chapter. As our homes have evolved, so too has the concept of a formal dining room. Most dining sets are stored in kitchens nowadays but sometimes they are in sideboards or cabinets too, and we want to ensure we don't overlook them as we don't have a chapter dedicated to a dining room. Ask yourself the following:

- Do you have inherited crockery that's never used taking up valuable space?

- Is it time to start using the 'special' crockery every day so you can enjoy it?
- Do you have a cabinet with drinks or spirits going back decades that you rarely drink, but feel you should keep hold of in case a guest wants it?
- Do you have placemats, tablecloths or napkins that are past their best or never used?
- Do you have cutlery that needs to be polished before use, so it never sees the light of day?

Only you will know whether keeping items for special or occasional use makes sense, but do make time as part of this project to evaluate whether the stuff you are keeping warrants the space it is taking up in your home.

BOARD GAMES, CARD GAMES AND JIGSAWS

If you are a committed board and card game kind of person, or a jigsaw lover, the chances are you will have a designated spot somewhere in your living area close at hand for them. Now, the issue with these things is that they are large and are often missing pieces.

Your decision-making ought to be based around how important these things are to you in your life and whether you have ample space to store them. Ask yourself:

- Does the frequency of your board and card game play or jigsaw making justify the space they take up?
- Are all the games age appropriate for your household?
- Are you sure all the games and jigsaws have all their pieces?
- If you have more games or jigsaws than you have space, can they be relocated elsewhere in the home?
- Would you be willing to split up the games into alternative storage pouches that will take up less space?

Do a thorough assessment of your board games, card games and jigsaws to make sure you are making best use of the space you have to store them. Be mindful that if you donate games, they should be carefully checked to ensure they are complete.

MEDIA – CDS, DVDS, VINYL AND VIDEO GAMES

There are three options when it comes to decluttering physical media, such as CDs, DVDs, vinyl and video games:

1. **You can decide to keep your 'collection' intact.** (It may be useful to refer back to the information about collections in the books chapter on p. 172 to help you determine whether this is the right decision for you.)
2. **You can decide to declutter your media in its entirety** and rely on streaming services.
3. **You can look at each individual component** of your media and pare it right down using recognisable decluttering questions.

Deciding whether to keep any media in physical form is such a huge choice. It's fair to say we could make the decision not to keep a single physical DVD, CD or record and still have access to more music, films, TV and games than we could ever realistically consume in a lifetime. But that doesn't mean that we *should* let go of all the physical copies of media we have bought over the years. It's a personal choice. And even if you decide yourself that your days of keeping copies of physical media are over, that doesn't mean other people in your household will agree.

Many people made a decision a couple of decades ago that CDs were the way forward. Some (not all) of those people are now lamenting the loss of their records now that vinyl has had a recent revival. It's so tough to predict what may happen in the future, so when we are decluttering, we need to be mindful that the decisions we make today are well intended and the right ones for here and now with the information we had available at the time.

But, if you have decided to plump for option 3 (paring down your collection), here are some questions that will help you in your quest for less:

- Will you ever watch, listen or play this again?
- Do you have duplicates?
- Is this in good enough condition to play?
- Is it age appropriate?

- Do you have this available in an alternative format?
- Are you struggling to contemplate splitting up your 'collection'?
- Are you willing to let go of CD or DVD cases to save space?

Decluttering media is a tricky decision for many people, so spend some time thinking about what the best solution is for your family. There are options out there to make some money from selling media so be sure to do your research. Often, selling is more time-consuming than it is lucrative though, so do factor that into your exit planning.

NOTEBOOKS

Over the years we've found that most people have their one 'thing' when it comes to clutter. That one thing they just can't walk past in a shop without buying. We've talked about clothes, we've talked about make-up, we've talked about books, but we've not yet talked about notebooks. It's such a funny old thing but some people just LOVE a notebook. Bullet journals, A4 jotters, diaries, soft cover notebooks, Filofaxes, planners – whatever you need to document, there's a different type of notebook to help you do so.

But many notebooks just sit there looking pretty and gathering dust. The first page or two may be filled in, but that's where the content stops. There was just something about that notebook that didn't work for us. It could well be that we already have several other designated notebooks for the same purpose.

Far be it from us to dictate whether or not you have more notebooks than you need, but our job is to ask the questions and challenge you, so if you're a diehard notebook lover (you know who you are!) then these questions are for you:

- Do you have a favoured type of notebook that you return to again and again?
- Do you buy notebooks in an attempt to make yourself more organised?
- Do you have notebooks you have gathered as free gifts that just don't deliver what they need to?
- Do you simply have more notebooks than you could ever use?

If you determine that enough is enough and it's time to shed some of your notebooks, they can go to a new home. If you have only used one or two pages, you can neatly slice the used pages out and the charity shop should be delighted to accept them. If you are determined to work through your excess, be sure to make a commitment to yourself that no new notebooks can be bought until you have worked your way through your inventory. Shop from home!

STATIONERY

There has been a monumental shift in our stationery usage over the past decade. The digital age means that we are not putting hard copy documents together like we used to. We barely write any more because all our communication is done via email. Those paper clips that we couldn't do without a few years ago are now pushed to the back of drawers, unloved and unused.

That said, there are still some things we do use, so we do need a basic supply of certain items, but it's the excessive volumes that we don't need. We regularly see envelopes in their hundreds, large containers of bulldog clips from the days when we needed to hold together a 60-page document, reams of plastic wallets to insert into ring binders to avoid tearing. The need for these things has reduced dramatically, therefore our supplies need to reflect that. The problem is that we feel they have a usefulness, so we are reluctant to let go.

Here are some questions to encourage you to live with less when it comes to stationery:

- Do you need stationery scattered in multiple areas of the home or is one central area sensible?
- Do you have a stationery item that has lain untouched for years?
- How many letters do you post that have a need for an envelope?
- Do you have empty ring binders waiting for their next use?
- Have you done a pen check lately to see what works and what doesn't?

Once again, take your time with stationery. Just because it *could* be useful at some point doesn't mean it should take up valuable space in your home that could be used for something way more useful. Say goodbye to the treasury tags and ink cartridges from your school days to allow space for something you can really use and enjoy here and now.

Be honest with yourself, be ruthless with your excess and enjoy the process. Checking whether a pen still writes might be a mindless task, but it can be super satisfying to find out everything is fit for purpose.

WRAPPING AND CARDS

We all need a little selection of wrapping paper, gift bags and cards we can draw upon when we are celebrating someone's special occasion. But again, the volumes need to be kept in perspective. Gift bags and wrapping paper are awkward to store and we almost always have way too many because we have also started to repurpose ones we get from other people.

Everyone's situation is completely different. If you have a large family or friendship group or you are firmly in that period of your life where it feels like you are wrapping a gift for a child in your child's class every weekend, you are going to need a little more than an average household.

But if you are more of an experience over stuff kind of person when it comes to gift giving, the chances of you getting through your backstock of cards and wrapping is slim. So, tap into realism, get ruthless with anything that's past its best, and don't be reluctant to donate your excess to charity. Here are some questions to help:

- Are all the card supplies you have ones you would actually send?
- Are some of the gift bags you have past their best?
- If you look at how many gifts or cards you need to send in a year, how does the amount you have stored compare?
- Even though you have supplies at home, do you find yourself grabbing new cards or wrapping at the store because you are not sure what you already have at home?

If you don't have oodles of space in your home, you need to keep your supplies to an absolute minimum and use clever storage so they don't overtake the space.

BATTERIES AND BULBS

It's always useful to have spare batteries and bulbs, but if you don't have the luxury of a bulk-storage area for them (such as a utility room or a designated space in your kitchen), your battery and bulb supplies may be in your living room.

First things first, you need to know what equipment, lights or lamps you have and what types of battery or bulbs you need. This may seem basic but, trust us, in our day-to-day work, we have found bulbs dating back decades and batteries that are years past their usefulness.

Again, this is a project and a half so take your time. It's a bit like putting the pieces of a puzzle together and you are going to need a plan to execute it. There's no point in *thinking* that you have something that needs a small bayonet bulb; you need to *know* for certain.

Invest in a battery tester to make sure your batteries are still functional and shake those bulbs to make sure the filaments are still intact. You may need to test some out in your lamps or light fittings because old bulbs have a nasty habit of being mixed up with new when you are replacing them. A helper, a ladder and a piece of paper and pen (to keep track of things you need to action) are going to be very helpful in this project.

If you do have excess stock, use a giveaway app to pass them on to a household that will use them. And for those that you are keeping, it's containerisation all the way.

ORNAMENTS, CANDLES AND PLANTS

Sometimes the very things that are designed to enhance a room completely detract from it. Pay careful attention to the ornaments, candles, plants, photo frames and pictures you have in your space to ensure you enjoy what they bring to your living room.

On p. 190 we talked about clutter blindness. Often, we overlook these kinds of objects because they are designed to be ornamental rather than functional, but it's important to pay close attention to both the volumes and quality of the things you choose to look at every day.

In Chapter 12 we are going to talk about sentimental items but, for now, here are a couple of things to consider with the less sentimental of our ornaments:

- Are your candles past their best or burnt out?
- Do your ornaments look curated or are they a mishmash of random things? Less is more when it comes to ornamental.
- Are all your house plants in good condition or do they need some TLC?
- Are your dried flowers faded or full of dust?
- Are photos in proper frames or are they loose and curled up at the edges?

Often the things we have decided to put front and centre in our homes outlive the joy they bring because we have seen them too often. Don't be afraid to rotate new ornaments for old to keep your room looking and feeling fresh.

WIRES AND CORDS

Arguably one of the most difficult things to declutter with confidence is wires, cables and cords. We are heavily reliant these days on charging cables for power and transfer cables to move media from one device to another. Often these cables become separated from their devices because the cables are seldom used. They are decades old with little to no labelling to help us in our quest. Cables move through generations at a rate of knots. Different people in our households have different devices. Cables get left in plug sockets all over the house. All in all, it's a veritable nightmare!

And if you dare to venture into the 'cable' box, it leaves you cold. How on earth can we literally and figuratively unravel years' worth of rogue cables and be confident that we are keeping the things we do need and letting go of the things we don't? Honestly, it's not easy. It involves trying to match devices and cables together, asking other people in the household to get involved and, once we are deep into the project, relying on internet searches to try and work out what's what. And all that involves time, energy and, most of all, patience.

In terms of advice, the best we can offer is to make sure you don't have this gargantuan task again in a few years' time, so be sure to future-proof your system. Invest in some cable labels and write on each and every wire you identify and keep what device it's for.

As a project, this one can stand alone. Do it after the rest of your living room is orderly. Be committed, be patient and be thorough; don't just shove all the wires back into the box and ignore them. Your future self will thank you for it, trust us! (Oh, and if you do work out a magic process for unravelling the cable spaghetti, do let us in on the secret.)

THE MISSING CATEGORIES

There may be a couple more categories that you are expecting to be included in this book, but we wanted to give you the heads up as to why we won't be covering them here. Toys, paperwork and craft are an absolute minefield when it comes to the emotional and practical considerations. In fact, each of these categories could be a whole book in itself. The decluttering and organising of toys is intrinsically linked to parenting and we're not experts. Getting your craft supplies under control involves a level of knowledge of crafting we just don't have. Paperwork is most certainly within our field of expertise but is too extensive for this book. For some basic pointers to help you tackle your paperwork see the appendix on page 247.

What we will say is that by now you have a much deeper understanding of the emotions that have held you back in the past, so tap into the knowledge you now have and attribute it to your toy, craft or paperwork clutter as necessary. You've got this!

Organisation and Storage

FURNITURE

On p. 190, when looking at the emotions involved in decluttering a living room, the ones we asked you to think about were largely evaluative and we'd like you to cast your mind back now. Take a long, hard look at this multifunctional space and, now that you are left with only those things that you use, need and love, make a further assessment as to whether the furniture and storage in this space is actually sensible for the things you have decided to keep. The living room should be a place first and foremost to relax but, of course, we need to store things in here too.

When we are looking at living room storage, we need to focus on creating a space where form and function blend seamlessly. We often have a surplus of furniture in the living room, which can add to the feeling of overwhelm. Removing pieces of furniture we no longer need can really open up a space, so now you have a better feel for what will be staying in here, is there anything furniture or storage wise that is not working and can be replaced? One of the best feelings in the world when decluttering is letting go of an excess of furniture that has been housing our excess of stuff.

Take a look at your shelf or bookcase storage. Are you utilising vertical space where you can? Instead of two smaller bookcases, can you swap to one larger one that stands taller but still maximises your storage? Can you add single shelves on to a wall to store books or ornaments? Would an ottoman help you to store blankets you use on an occasional basis? If multiple TV remotes are a problem, can you containerise them to keep them neater?

CONTAINERS AND ORGANISING SOLUTIONS

Are you using cable ties to minimise cable spaghetti? If you have chosen to keep DVDs, CDs or vinyl, do they need to be on display or can you keep them somewhere that is accessible but doesn't detract from the aesthetic needs of this room?

Boxes and containers are going to be your friend. Often in a living room, we have bookcase storage that is not that deep. Utilise narrow boxes with lids that stack and are all the same or a co-ordinating colour or pattern. If you have loose papers or magazines, will magazine files help? Be sure to measure carefully before investing in storage boxes, so you can be sure you are maximising the storage space you have available.

Categorisation and zoning should loosely follow the categories we mentioned earlier (on pp. 197–206) and volumes of each of these categories should now be minimal, so there will be no need for elaborate zoning. If you feel like you need more visible reminders for where things live by using labels, choose ones that focus on aesthetics more than function.

So, it's time to start putting things back into their containers and choose their designated spot. At this point you will undoubtedly have some sentimental items you need to sort through, so keep them to one side as that's going to be our next project.

The Finishing Touches

Getting your living room to this stage is going to feel incredible. It is a key room to get right so be sure to give it the final care and attention it needs. Vacuum and dust the room thoroughly, including any soft furnishings, so your room looks its absolute best.

Anything you have set aside to donate needs to be popped in the car or hallway with a specific plan to get it to its destination.

And now for a counter-intuitive piece of advice. Does your room need any finishing touches? Are you missing a picture here or a cushion there? Although encouraging you to buy things doesn't often form part of our advice, you will now feel so proud and connected to your new space that you may want to add those finishing touches that will elevate your living room and increase your enjoyment of it. Just be sure that any additions you make are well thought through and intentional.

Take a photo of your room and show off all your hard work. If there are other people in your household, the accomplishment of this room is a huge step forwards and they should be feeling excited about the changes too. Enjoy it together.

Grab a cup of tea, relax in your new space, take a few days off and then be ready for the last area we are going to tackle, which is sentimental items. We've saved the best till last (honestly!).

TAKE A MOMENT

It's time to reflect on the strides we have made in our decluttering journey now that we are nearing the end of our Phase One. Ask yourself the following:

- Can you identify how you feel now you have finished all the key rooms in your home?
- Are other people in your home sharing in your delight?
- Do you feel differently about your home now you can see things more clearly?
- Are you proud of the progress you have made emotionally and practically?

12

Sentimental items

'Choose quality over quantity, always.'

Our decluttering muscle is now stronger than ever, our clutter is shrinking, but throughout all the rooms we have covered so far we have had a consistent piece of advice: leave the sentimental items till later in your journey. Later is now here and we're just about to board the bus. This leg of the journey starts today.

As we work through this stage, we suggest you take your time, savour the memories and devote yourself to this life-affirming trip down memory lane. Most of us are sentimental souls, after all (we know we are). We have families, we have friends, we have had childhoods, relationships, careers, holidays, big birthdays – and all of these things, and many more occasions besides, bring with them a whole heap of memories.

We hope more than anything that the lion's share of your memories are happy ones. There's no doubt that life has a habit of throwing curveballs our way sometimes and the memories of turbulent times can be tough to bear. Nevertheless, the things we have kept from those tougher times can be living proof of us having overcome adversity and that deserves acknowledgement, too.

But, most of the time, the things we choose to keep as physical reminders of our past are all about the good times. And we need to savour those good times, enjoy our memories and ensure they form a special part of our current lives. In order for that to happen we need to separate the wheat from the chaff. We need to evaluate those things that immediately give us that warm fuzzy feeling inside and take us back to a poignant moment we loved. Having things scattered around your home, buried in that leather trunk in your garage, hiding at the bottom of your bedroom drawer underneath your socks, or stuffed in a box on the top of your wardrobe with your travel supplies, does not allow us to see these things, let alone enjoy them and enjoy a sentimental rush. The time to change that is now.

In other rooms we have learned to understand and acknowledge how our emotional connection to things has held us back from making the right choice. At this point in your journey, we are urging you to embrace these emotions rather than challenge them. Relive sentimental moments and embrace the things that represent them. Recognise them for the truly special times they have been. Sentimentality is a good thing. Our homes would be bland and lacking personality without it.

As you work through the process of decluttering your sentimental items, you'll find that some of the things you always thought were sentimental actually aren't. There will be things from other people, things that evoke negativity and things that you have no recollection of at all. And we need to work through the negative or neutral stuff to reconnect with the positive. This part of your decluttering journey is all about finding quality over quantity. Sentimental gems have a hierarchy and it is our task to find the diamonds in among the cubic zirconia.

It is for a very good reason that we urge you to leave your sentimental items till the end of the process. You need to come to terms with, and challenge, more basic emotions way before you start to make a decision about whether you are ready to let go of something pertaining to your late father or your children. But we've been honing your decluttering muscle throughout this book and we hope that the practice you've had in making decisions up to now means you can face your sentimental items with a sense of control, and an understanding of the kind of decisions that make sense for you.

In most areas of the home there are countless no-brainer decisions, but that is not the case with sentimental items. With sentiment comes complexity and depth of thought. As every home is different, every life is different. You may feel thankful, you may feel blessed, you may feel wistful, you may feel aggrieved. Life shows up in so many different ways that it is hard to give targeted advice about what should provide the cornerstone of your sentimental collection.

But if there is one piece of advice we will give it's this: seek out that warm fuzzy feeling and cling on to it for dear life. Precious memories are everything.

The thinking

Emotional Preparation

As you can imagine, sentimentality is a complex beast. Each and every type of sentimental category has different types of emotion associated with it, but there are some overarching ones to think about, too.

QUALITY OVER QUANTITY

Let's jump straight into a concept that arguably underpins every decluttering decision we make in our homes. Whether sentimental or not, every item we choose to keep in our homes should be analysed based on its quality. We should evaluate the impact something has in our lives. It could serve a practical purpose or indeed, in the case of sentimental items, it could be something you just love having around you.

For example, when your toddler comes home from nursery every single day with a brand-new spaghetti-covered, glittery work of art, does every masterpiece need to stay? When you have hundreds of elastic-bound bundles of cards from every birthday you and your family members have had, can you truthfully claim they are all equally special? If you are running in 10ks and half marathons several times a year, does each medal demonstrate the same sense of pride and accomplishment?

There's no doubt that a child's painting, a birthday card or a running medal is special, but are they all equally evocative and can we truly enjoy the memory when there are sometimes hundreds more where that came from?

WHOSE MEMORY IS IT?

One of the toughest parts of a sentimental sort is when you have items, often several boxes of things, that you have inherited. If you are bereaved, it can be tough to move past the notion that everything relating to the person you have lost is sentimental.

Often, when we are tasked with clearing out the home of someone who has died, we are not ready to make difficult decisions about letting go of things that are highly charged, so we box them up and vow to deal with them later. Weeks pass, months pass, sometimes years pass, and the items are still there waiting to be tackled, but when we decide the time is right we feel so discombobulated that it becomes almost impossible to make the right decision.

Our focus, as always, should be on quality over quantity, but we want to introduce something else for you to ponder. We've mentioned the concept of a warm fuzzy feeling being a barometer with which to gauge how special something is to us. Let's use a suitcase of old cards that your mum had kept for years as an example. As you start to look through these items, you do not even recognise the names of the people who sent them. You feel no connection, no warm fuzzy feeling, but you still struggle to make the decision to let them go. If the item you are looking at belongs to someone else and evokes no memory at all, why would you keep it? Are you keeping it out of guilt? Do you feel that by letting go of the item you are doing a disservice to the person you have lost?

When working through the belongings of other people, it's vital to continually ask yourself the question, 'Whose memory is it?' You do not need to keep generations' worth of items just because you feel a sense of responsibility. Your mum had her memories during her life, you will have your own and generations below you will have theirs, all equally valid but personal and disparate. Sentimental items, by their nature, need to evoke sentiment. Otherwise they are just more stuff.

We'd like to throw into the mix one more thing to consider. If you are lucky enough to still have the opportunity to invest time into sharing stories and memories with your loved ones by looking through photos, letters or cards together, make it a priority to schedule time into your diary for this. Spending time with the older generations talking through their memories is priceless. This time together adds a whole new dimension to the things you may one day inherit, and your sentimental sorting will be more poignant and have the added bonus of the clarity of knowing the things you are keeping are extra special and why.

NAVIGATING NEGATIVITY

Now we come to the important question of whether we should keep things that harbour negative associations for us. Our general advice would be no, but we understand that alongside turbulent times come complex thoughts and fears, so it is clearly a hugely personal choice.

If you have gone through a difficult break-up and have unkind communication in a file in your attic, for example, is it helpful to chance upon that letter during your general decluttering? It could immediately derail you and take you back to a dark place. If you have gone through a tough spell at work that led to a tribunal or meetings with HR, do you need to be reminded of the turmoil you suffered?

Often we keep these items because we feel so incredulous that such a traumatic thing happened to us that we feel a need to retain the evidence as a kind of personal proof. Sometimes there are legal reasons why something needs to be retained, but if that isn't the case, ask yourself why you are clinging on to something. What will you gain from retaining this memory?

The harsh fact is that the only effect chancing upon an item like this will have is a negative one. We cannot give you a definitive answer whether to keep or let go of an item like this but we would urge you to take some time out to think about the pros and cons. If you offload the negativity from your life, you will most certainly feel like a heavy weight has been lifted, but equally you may not be ready. Just consider the possibility of letting go at this stage, and if you're not ready, you can come back to it in another phase of decluttering.

SHARING THE LOVE

Sorting out your sentimental items provides an opportunity for you to reconnect with people from your past. Back in the day, letter writing was a major form of communication and many letters are absolute gold dust that take us right back to a cherished moment in time. The content of a letter was almost the olden-day equivalent of a Facebook post – an opportunity to share what you were doing, what you were thinking and what you were planning. When you re-read letters from decades ago, they are often such special memories, but if we return to the concept of 'whose memories are they' on p. 213, a letter is often the musings of the person who wrote it rather than the recipient. So perhaps what we choose to do with these should take a slightly different path?

This deep dive into your past and the items you have kept provides an opportunity for you to share the love. Offer to send either the original or copies of these letters to your best friend who meticulously wrote to you each and every week of your uni days, so they too can enjoy their thoughts from that era. Pop copies of old photobooth photos over to the people who belly-laughed with you every weekend as a teenager. Show your kids their Kings and Queens project work from Year 4. A sentimental project doesn't need to be a solitary project. This is your chance to share the love. And that's the very reason why we've left this project till last, so you can spend as much time as you need to enjoy these precious memories and shared moments without worrying about the clutter that would have been waiting for you in your bedroom.

As you embark on sentimental decluttering, you will undoubtedly be taken to a whole new place. We always find things we had forgotten we had and unearth things we thought we had lost when decluttering, but this part of the journey is at another level.

We will be going into even more detail about some of the key categories of sentimental items that exist in your home but, for now, think about the main emotions associated with them:

- Do you feel ready to admit that you have kept too many sentimental items in your home? Are you favouring things from the past and taking up valuable space you need for the here and now?
- Do you have things in your home you feel little or no connection to because they have been inherited?
- Do you know you have things around from a difficult time in your life and you now feel you want to assess their validity in your current life?
- Are you looking forward to reconnecting with old friends through shared memories?

This project may take some time but that's OK. All of our decluttering so far has been building up to this opportunity to enjoy the things we have kept. Our homes should make us happy and getting this project right will propel us in the right direction.

Goal Setting

Setting a big-picture goal for your sentimental items is trickier than in other rooms of your home, but nevertheless consider the following possibilities:

- You want to pass things on to your loved ones now and share the memories and the meaning behind the items.

- You have a special event coming up and are trying to collate a scrapbook or photobook.
- You are downsizing or moving home and have limited space for sentimental items.
- You feel some of your sentimental objects may have value and you want to recoup some money.
- You have been waiting to do a project like this and you want to make best use of this window of opportunity.

So, what's your why? What is going to be the thing that drives you to work through your sentimental items? This part of the decluttering journey will feel different to some of the other areas you have worked in, but that big-picture goal is no less vital. Keep a record of your goal somewhere so you can refer back to it later.

Planning Section by Section

Have a think about logistics. Where are all your sentimental items? You may have things waiting patiently in boxes you kept to one side as you worked through all the rooms in your home. There may be boxes on top of wardrobes, under beds, in kids' rooms, in basements, in attics or in garages. You name it, there may be a sentimental item there.

It may be sensible to work through your items box by box or you may have space to gather all the boxes together. If you need help getting your boxes all together, ask for that help now. It's essential to assess the scale of your sentimental items before you begin because you don't want an extra surprise sentimental box to rear its head later down the line when you thought the project was complete.

Sentimental items span all manner of things, from clothes to toys, from medals to certificates, so referring to the 'Decluttering category by category' section on p. 219 will allow you to retain control of your project and, if possible, work section by section. Take it at a pace that will work for your timescale and your home.

Physical Preparation and Logistics

The length of time a sentimental project will take is very dependent on the volume of things you have kept over the years. As we've mentioned, we want you to take your time and enjoy the process, so meticulous planning is key here.

Do you have several windows of opportunity over the next few days or weeks? This project is likely to span multiple pockets of time. Think carefully about when you are going to do this and where. There will be a lot of gathering like with like at first, so do you have a table you can use to sort? Some of the things you come across will be old, antique even, and may involve special handling, so a table or a designated surface you can keep in position for as long as the project takes will be super handy.

You will (as always) need bin bags, in particular, ones that you can recycle your paper into, as many of the things within a sentimental project are paper-based. Have some temporary storage boxes you can use when you are pre-sorting too, then when you have a better idea of what your long-term needs are, you can buy more permanent storage solutions.

Do you have an idea of who might benefit from some of the items you choose to let go of? Charity shops, family members or giveaway apps are all contenders. If you feel you have a good handle on the types of things you might come across at this stage, do your homework on where the potential outlets for your stuff might be.

And, even though a photo is not quite so important for this project, it will do no harm at all so snap your progress as you work through things.

The doing

How and Where to Get Started

In all honesty, sentimental items are often in such a muddle there's no right or wrong place to start. If you have been able to gather all your sentimental items from all over the house you will have the luxury of being able to see them together in one go, and you may have some basic order already established. So, now identify those categories that have the biggest volumes and start there. It's important, if possible, to see the volumes decrease to keep yourself motivated and moving forwards. But, more often than not, your sentimental items are just a random heap of stuff mixed together in a box, so you just need to take it one box at a time and categorise as you go.

Having said that, if you have children or other family members who are tackling their stuff too, it's worth working through things person by person, and then category by category.

If you are embarking on photographs as part of your sentimental project, view them as a whole separate category so you don't get bogged down in the details. We recommend you come back to photos after you have done all the other categories of sentimental items.

For now, concentrate on opening up those bags and boxes and start to make some decluttering decisions. We're going to talk through all the things to consider category by category now.

Decluttering Category by Category

CARDS

Most of us have at least a card or two that we have been given in our sentimental collections. But some of us have hundreds, even thousands. If you keep every card from every occasion for every person in your home, that's a lot of birthdays and a lot of special occasions! You'll be overrun with cards before you know it.

It's fair to say that some people are extra thoughtful when it comes to sending cards and others are just sending them more out of a sense of obligation. Think about this when deciding which cards to keep and which to let go of. You will know when a card is extra special. Its special status may be related to the person or it may have been a very poignant occasion.

Keeping every card we ever receive does not allow us to adhere to the quality over quantity rule. If you have made a decision that you have too many cards and want to declutter some, let's give you some pointers on where to start.

If the card has a simple 'To Ingrid, Happy Birthday, Love Lesley' message, is that truly special? Think carefully about the sentiment that sits behind the card. Does it feel thoughtful, considered and unique?

Let's say you get 10 cards for each birthday and you started saving them when you were 20 and you're now 55. That's a whopping 350 cards for just one annual occasion. Once you add in other members of your family and other occasions too, it runs to thousands. To curtail the volumes, would you be willing to only keep cards from big birthdays and lose the interim ones, for example?

Do you love a funny card or a photocard? We all have our own favourite type, so work out what that is for you and try to find those among the others. Keep the quality over quantity rule firmly front and centre in your mind at all times and, before you know it, you'll be making the right decisions on your volumes.

So, you need to make a plan about how many cards you are keeping from your current keepsakes and then also commit to an ongoing plan of action.

Once you have whittled down your card numbers, how are you going to store them or use them? Craft projects, a digital capture of the message or simply gathered together into a box or folder works well. Do you want to store cards by person, by occasion, by decade? There are lots of decisions to make but each choice will take you closer to your goal of being able to truly enjoy the ones you have left.

LETTERS

The age you are is largely going to determine how many letters you have in your possession. In the pre-mobile phone and pre-internet era, letter writing was the cheapest way to keep in touch and so it was well utilised. Trust us when we say, the letters will take you right back to a time and place that you (hopefully) have fond memories of.

Working through letters takes time and ought to be savoured. We will learn things about our family, friends and partners we may have completely forgotten about. They will make us laugh, cry and everything in between. Love letters sent from your partner in the early days, letters from your mum keeping you caught up with the latest hometown gossip, letters from your best friend with each little detail of their latest love affair. Letters are precious little moments of personal history and to be honest, unless there's really good reason, we believe they should be kept and savoured.

But not all letters are equal, so when you're looking for ones to let go of, look for the obvious. Is the ink still legible? Do you remember the person they were from? Do they contain things that are painful to read? Removing the envelopes can remove some of the excess paper but equally the envelopes can be as nostalgic as the letter itself, and also serve to protect the letter.

Don't forget to share the love too. If you are still in contact with the person who sent it, pop over a copy to them or even the original if you choose not to keep it. It might just be the best gift you've ever given them.

How are you going to organise the letters you are keeping? By person, by decade or by event are all possible options.

Storage wise, keep things simple. Use files, folders or wallets and if you want your personal letters to remain private, keep them away from prying eyes.

ORNAMENTS AND TRINKETS

Ornaments and trinkets tend to be, or have been, on display in your home for a while, so although these are often just there for aesthetic reasons, some are sentimental too. You may have already looked at these items as part of your standard room decluttering, but if not, make the time to think about how your ornaments and trinkets have made their way to your home and whether they are worth keeping hold of.

Do you pick up souvenirs from your holidays or do other people bring you gifts from theirs? Have you got fridge magnets galore? Have you inherited ornaments throughout the years? Do you have things sitting on your mantelpiece that have real value? Are your ornaments things that your children and grandchildren have made in school? Do you have a collection of something that has grown and grown?

Sometimes the things that stare back at us from mantelpieces, windowsills and shelves are the easiest things to declutter. We have just never really paid them much attention because we have become clutter blind (*see* p. 190 for more on this).

Here are some ideas to encourage you to let some ornaments go:

- If someone brought you a gift from a place you have never been, is it even sentimental for you?
- If your children or grandchildren are gifting you the fruits of their artistic labour, how long is long enough to display it?
- If your friends and family know you have a collection you love, have you received ones over the years that you wouldn't have bought (and displayed) yourself?
- Are you willing to split your collection down and choose only the most special or are you indeed ready to let go of the whole collection?
- Do you have something on display you are keeping because you think it is valuable? Do your research so you are sure and determine whether or not it is better for you to sell or display.
- Have your tastes in decor changed and you favour a more streamlined look that your ornaments no longer fit into.

When you've decided what you're keeping, you need to ensure that the things you are choosing to place front and centre in your life are given the best chance to shine. They need to look intentional. Curate your collection carefully and don't be afraid to add in additional wall storage if it's needed.

CERTIFICATES AND AWARDS

When we receive a certificate or award we naturally feel a sense of pride because we have obviously put in great effort to achieve something, but there's a marked difference between a 100-metre swimming certificate and a university degree certificate. There are a couple of things to consider when you are trying to separate the quality from the quantity.

The passage of time naturally means we are evolving. That swimming certificate we received at eight years old may now be largely irrelevant because we continued on our swimming journey and achieved 200 metres and then a mile and so on. Equally, if you have since become a celebrated swimmer, each of those certificates marks a special moment of your rise to stardom and may need to be retained.

When we have recently achieved something that we have worked hard for, the certificate or award means everything to us because the sense of accomplishment is so fresh, but gradually that accolade may become less important. The certificates you encounter that have just become administrative rather than sentimental are the ones to weed out.

You may feel you want to keep every certificate you've ever received and that's fine. But don't be held back thinking you *need* to keep certificates as a legal record of achievements. There are very few things that will be required by employers other than your educational qualifications. No one needs to see that Manual Handling Certificate from 1995. If it's not special, let it go!

Once you've decided what you want to keep, think about storage options too. Display books are great and will keep everything together. Do also think about creating digital versions of your certificates and awards as well. You can easily scan or photograph certificates, which will allow for easy retrieval should you need them.

MEDALS, TROPHIES AND PLAQUES

Closely linked to certificates and awards are medals, trophies and plaques. While they also exist to reward hard work, commitment and achievement, the difference is that these are physical objects rather than pieces of paper, so the need to keep them to a minimum and favour quality over quantity is even greater.

Think about the passage of time and whether your sense of pride has waned. If you or a child has really immersed themselves in an activity, then medals and plaques can really mount up and it is a very tough decision to let some go.

Try and distinguish between those that were given out just for taking part from those that reward a greater sense of achievement. A trophy given out to the whole team just for being in the team is very different to receiving the Coaches' Player of the Year Award, for example.

In terms of storage options, particularly for medals, there are some clever display options on the market today that will allow you to show your things off with pride.

We have largely talked about sports trophies, but of course military medals also exist. These tend to be kept and enjoyed, but do remember to ask yourself whose memories are they?

CHILDREN'S ARTWORK

Now we come to a particularly tricky category: children's artwork. If you are ever the recipient of your children's masterpieces then a whole new dimension of sentiment is added in. Our children are arguably the most precious things we have in our lives and the speed at which they grow and develop is mind-blowing. We feel connection, pride and humour about the things they create but, it's fair to say, if we don't have a plan to deal with artwork, you can become overrun, particularly if you have multiple primary-age children.

While we are not advocates of decluttering other people's things, when it comes to primary-age children we have input in most areas of their lives as parents and we ought to be in a position to be able to make the right decision about whether or not to involve them in decluttering. Younger primary-age children do not have the full range of information and emotional maturity required to make a sensible decision about how many things they should keep. Only you will know whether involving them in these decluttering decisions will be a help or a hindrance. Some children will want to keep everything, others will be beyond ruthless in what they throw away, so your job is to find balance and teach them valuable life skills along the way.

We do suggest you need to get a little ruthless when it comes to the backlog of artwork you may have dotted around the house or in boxes, and you also need a plan to keep things under control going forwards.

As with all sentimental items, all paintings are not created equal. The ones that allow you a window into their world are the special ones – the ones that show their true personality. In addition, pictures of the whole family in all their glory can provide laughs decades down the line. These are the types of gems that ought to be treasured.

Declutter now to clear the backlog and then make a plan to keep them under control from here on in. Involve your child in choosing which artwork they would like on display this week and be clear that some things will not be kept forever. This is hard stuff. It involves negotiation and has a bearing on the relationship with your child. Some children are fine with letting go and some children will cling on for dear life to their things. (After all, they've learned the art of holding on to stuff from the masters!) You might get a tantrum thrown into the mix that you really don't have the energy for. But it is necessary to take control and have a plan you agree on otherwise you will have hundreds of pieces of kids' artwork before you know it. We're focusing on safeguarding the quality and letting go of the quantity.

The good news is that displaying kids artwork is a universal problem and where there is a problem, some clever person has had the foresight to find a solution. There are companies that you can post your artwork to and they will curate them digitally into a book. There are frames that allow you to swap kids' artwork over easily week by week. A quick internet search will provide some inventive and enriching solutions.

So, the message here is simple: you can't keep everything; you need to determine the real gems and let the rest go.

SCHOOLBOOKS

Schoolbooks are tricky as they are a tangible throwback to the creativity we or our children had growing up. But our school days bring with them a huge volume of work. We were writing, drawing, spelling and creating each and every day of our school lives, and that brings with it a lot of physical paper and books. We will most likely want to keep some, but not all, schoolbooks in a sentimental collection.

So how do we go about deciding quality over quantity? Typically the schoolbooks that feel most special are those that are creative. Knowing that your child nailed the difference between *there* and *their* in Year 3 or reading through some algebraic formulae isn't that exciting. Instead, it's in the creative subjects that a child's personality shines through. It is that story about what your child loved most about their seaside holiday or their thoughts about what they'd like to be when they grow up that you want to read in years to come. Looking back at things like this when your children have flown the nest is special. These are the books to keep. Don't be afraid to dismantle the book and extract the special stories or drawings. You don't need to keep a book intact for it to be special. It's almost like extracting a newspaper cutting. It will cut down on volumes and immediately take you to the premium content.

And if you're still firmly in schoolbook territory with your kids now, establish a pattern of going through all books at the end of each school year and asking them which they are most proud of and would like to keep.

COURSE NOTES

Fast-forward a few years beyond glitter paintings and pasta portraits and we move into course notes. Similar to children's artwork, our course notes capture educational progress throughout the years and this is, of course, something we can feel very connected to.

But what is it about these items that makes us keep hold of them? Pride is a large component of this again – you are proud of yourself for devoting care and attention to something and making a breakthrough at school or college. That concept can be difficult to let go of and you feel like you need the physical reminder. It is a snapshot of your personal history, especially if it is a university, school or work project you poured your heart and soul into.

There is also the possibility that you have unfinished business with a course you started and you have vowed to finish it one day. So the course notes are being kept for aspirational reasons. All these things are key components of our lives and the sentiment and emotion is strong.

Decluttering any sentimental items becomes pertinent when the volume is too overwhelming. You can choose to keep these items but be sure to challenge yourself with the item's usefulness to you going forwards. Tap into realism – will you ever look back at your philosophy dissertation when you now work in marketing? Even if you are still working in a relevant field, has the 50-year-old you amassed experience and knowledge that is far superior to that held by the 20-year-old you?

If there's that one special assignment that you can't bear to part with, contemplate the option of creating a digital version or, of course, reconnect with it, keep it and enjoy it. If it can be bound, think about adding it to your standard bookcase so you can chance upon it more often than if it were lying in a box.

CHILDREN'S CLOTHING

It's time to move on to clothes. You can be forgiven for looking at the first sleepsuit your new baby came out of hospital in, or your own christening gown, and feeling a huge sense of nostalgia. Children are special and we have fond memories of them over the years wearing different items of clothing.

But when we come across bags and bags of children's old clothes that we have struggled to part with, we need to look at why.

Here are some facts to help you consider your items:

- It's so much nicer to see the child's smiling face in a photograph wearing the clothing. This provides the context you need to take you back to that special moment. Maybe a photo is enough and you don't need the item itself?
- If you are keeping your child's first pair of shoes to hand down to your son or daughter, think back to whose memory is it? You're the one with the special memory of them walking around in them. They won't have any recollection. You might want to keep them but know that you are doing this for yourself.
- Keeping a small, curated collection of special clothes in a designated section of your wardrobe that you see regularly is way more impactful than having bags and bags of stuff in the basement.

- When your child is tiny, it's hard to think that you will ever get to a stage when the pair of jeans they wore at four years old will not be heart-warmingly special, but the passage of time is a powerful thing. At some point we will let go and there's a whole lifetime of memories still waiting to be made.

And by far the most important thing to remember is this: you have your photos to bring the clothing to life. You don't need all the physical items.

ADULT'S CLOTHING

Sentimental clothing is one of the trickiest categories to declutter. All the emotions relating to a standard wardrobe declutter (*see* pp. 91–96) still stand, but there is more to be discussed still with the sentimental items that we've chosen to keep. Wedding attire, concert T-shirts, sports shirts, clothes from someone who has died; if an item is related to a special occasion, event or person we cherished, often it is kept to one side for years.

But, sometimes, sentimental clothing threatens to hijack the space we have designated for our everyday clothes. Practical storage needs should always outweigh sentimental ones. But this is tough. Many people have enough storage to easily store some special items, but some people don't and that's when we need to evaluate the value attached to them, and whether we have an alternative option to keep that sentiment alive.

Again, we have photos to fall back on, although if these items go back decades, photographic evidence was way less common then than it is now. You may have something you kept from the day you got engaged and that's the only thing you have as a reminder.

Look at each and every item you are keeping and assess just how special it feels to you. If you have multiple items from a person who has died, for example, can you still evoke the special memories you feel with just one or two items? And put these items somewhere you can see and touch them. Have a designated section of your wardrobe, for example, where these can hang so you can connect with the sentiment regularly.

BROCHURES, PROGRAMMES, TICKETS AND LEAFLETS

Some of the most special and memorable moments in our lives relate to special events: theatre shows, concerts, theme parks and days out. All of these involve unique events that we enjoy and naturally want to remember for years to come.

Each event brings with it an option to acquire tickets, passes, brochures or leaflets. And chances are you have a few in your sentimental boxes. It may be that attending events like this is a rarity or it may be something you are doing with regularity. Maybe the first time you saw the *Lion King* in your twenties felt breathtaking but now you go to a theatre show several times a year, so it's just become less special over time. Is that receipt for a croissant in a bakery in Paris the thing that will become your main memory?

Whether or not you should keep memorabilia is a personal matter, but here are some questions to ask yourself as a basis for decluttering:

- Do you have photos or videos from the event?
- Has the purchase of merchandise just become a habit?
- Will having a programme of the theatre, cinema, show, concert or sports event make you remember it more?
- Is the entrance ticket enough or do you need the leaflet and the programme as well?
- Have you ever looked at them after you've attended the show?
- Are they gathering dust on a shelf?

It can be hard, but not impossible, to make what feels like a radical decision to declutter some or all of this type of memorabilia, and it's also important to make a resolution with yourself to stop the clutter at source too. If you decide to declutter some or all of your memorabilia collection, be sure not to buy or collect anything next time you attend an event.

CALENDARS, DIARIES AND JOURNALS

This category can be split into two different groups, so we'll look at both in turn.

Recording our appointments

The first group in this category are those calendars and diaries used for recording dates and appointments. A paper-based calendar is something that we typically hang on a wall or prop up on a desk as a practical reminder of what we are doing when. You can also use a paper diary for the same purpose. Many of us now choose to use a digital calendar instead, so the use of physical calendars and diaries is decreasing. In terms of whether or not these types of diary and calendar should be kept, there's very little need to, so most people choose to let them go.

The interesting thing is that many people who struggle to let go of physical calendars have never looked at their settings on their digital calendars to manage how far back records are retained, yet they keep the paper-based stuff for decades. You see, paper almost always trumps digital when we are being sentimental.

There can be situations where it might be useful to keep these paper records. Sometimes these items are required to be kept for work, for example, or you may want to keep a chronological record of medical appointments. Also be mindful of people who are ageing or struggling with elements of memory loss, as paper-based chronological records for these people can be very powerful and validating.

Recording our thoughts

The second group in this category is a very different type of diary: a diary to record our innermost thoughts, fears and aspirations. A journal in its various guises also does a similar thing. Now, who is not going to love turning back time to your teenage self to gain an insight into way back when?

The reality is, if you are a deep thinker who loves to put your positive thoughts into writing, the chances are you'll never let the diaries and journals go that reflect your journey through life and that's OK. As far as sentimental goes, these are A-list items. And kudos to you for recording your thoughts. We're pretty sure many of us wish we had done the same throughout our lives so we also had a thorough autobiographical representation that we could always cherish, and wouldn't need all this stuff to serve as reminders.

If, on the other hand, you would find the contents too painful, pop back to p. 214 to think about whether negative associations deserve a place in your sentimental life at all.

So, when it comes to working through that pile of calendars, diaries and journals, first separate out the practical ones from the sentimental ones and then gather them chronologically or thematically so you can rediscover and enjoy them in your leisure time.

SOFT TOYS

Now, we'd like to be able to sit here and direct all our thoughts on soft toys to those parents still very much in child-rearing mode, but the fact of the matter is that soft toys tend to reside in our homes long after the kids have flown the nest. So whether you have an abundance of soft toys that your children are still playing with or boxes of soft toys in a cupboard somewhere, we feel your pain: decluttering soft toys is hard. Why is this?

First, they're designed to look super cute. Second, the moment you see them you're taken right back to a precious time in your life. Third, the volumes of soft toys we amass over the years is colossal. Finally, they are not easy to pass on to a good home.

All these factors involved in something as simple as a Build-A-Bear or a Winnie the Pooh plush mean that homes all around the world have that bin bag full of soft toys that gets brought out periodically and then put straight back without anything heading to the donate pile.

But soft toys are big, bulky and dusty. When the time is right, we need to be able to make the right decision and let at least some go to create space for things that are more useful in our homes.

We've rarely seen a successful all-to-nothing declutter when it comes to soft toys. But what does seem to work is a phased approach. Ask your child (when we say child, that might be a 10-year-old or a strapping 36-year-old man) to help you come to some decluttering decisions. Agree on a percentage you feel comfortable to let go of, pin down a timescale and go for it. Your agreement may be to aim for 30 per cent of the (least sentimental) soft toys to go now, and then you'll return to it again in a year from now. Often that works.

And when it comes to donation, do your homework on your exit plan. If you know that your soft toy (or your child's) is going to be loved and cherished by its next owner, it smooths the transition hugely.

CHINA, GLASSWARE AND DINNER SERVICES

In days gone by, collecting every component of a dinner service from a gravy boat to a coffee pot, from a sugar bowl to a platter, was coveted and commonplace. These sets cost an absolute fortune, were front and centre of every wedding gift registry and often ran to 96-piece sets. They had pride of place in some kind of open glass cabinet and formed a very vivid part of many of our childhood memories.

So, when the time comes for that dinner service to be passed down the generations, it's a tough decision to let it go. Some people are more than happy, even delighted, to bring it into their homes and give it another life, but nowadays we typically have more stuff and less space and have to make compromises in what we choose to keep.

If you have space and love the dinner service, there's no issue, but what if you love the idea of retaining the memory but simply don't have the space?

We're looking to emote something when we pick up that piece of china: we want it to take us back to family memories from a different era. But we don't need 96 pieces of china to do that. One or two will suffice. You can retain the memory with one plate, one cup and saucer, or a gravy boat you bring out at Christmas. The purpose of it being sentimental is fulfilled and you are not taking up valuable space in your home for something you rarely use.

What's also important is never to keep things tucked away for best. Use the china for your afternoon cup of tea, have your Friday wine in the crystal glass. Yes there's a greater chance of it breaking but better to have loved and lost than to have never loved at all, as they say.

Making a decision about inherited china like this is hard but once you move past the idea that it has to be kept intact, you'll feel like you've done the right thing.

FURNITURE

When it comes to sentimental furniture, ruthless is the name of the game. You need to absolutely love something for it to warrant the large amount of space a piece of furniture takes up in your home.

If you inherit a piece of furniture that you love but does not work well in your current home, don't be afraid to make alterations. That brown sideboard from your grandma's house might look incredible with a lick of paint. There are lots of clever ways to mix the old with the new that means a piece of furniture can retain its sentimentality without becoming burdensome.

Other pieces of furniture that are kept for sentimental reasons are children's cots and beds. It's not easy to let go of such a special piece of furniture but if you choose to keep it you need to have a plan. Has your daughter committed to using it if she has a child, for example? If not, have the conversation so you can work out a sensible plan that means your treasured item has a second life.

Because furniture is sizable, you need to make the right decision. You see, you can choose to keep a letter or a card if you're not quite ready to make a decision yet (because keeping it is not going to make or break a house), but keeping furniture that doesn't fit is an entirely different matter.

FRAMED PHOTOGRAPHS AND PIECES OF ART

Hands up if you have a stack of photos or artwork that you have taken off your wall but is now sitting in your attic or basement? It will come as no surprise that you're not alone. In homes up and down the land there is a stash of frames the homeowners just can't let go of.

This is a classic example of delayed decisions that we spoke about back on p. 109. We decided that the painting or photograph no longer serves its purpose to us so we dutifully put it with all the others in the pile. But are we ever going to put back that family portrait when we've had an updated one that now has pride of place? Does it still seem feasible we will rehang our daughter's graduation photo when our grandchildren are now graduating?

When are we ever going to return to these pictures we have taken down and decide to put them back up? Is it the best decision for our homes and our decluttering journeys to have these things hanging around till the end of time?

If you are genuinely struggling to let go, here are some ideas:

- Think about removing frames to save space.
- Think about creating a gallery or montage wall so you can reinstate some of your special art or photos.
- If you are wondering whether something is valuable, make a specific plan to do your research.
- Check whether anyone else in your family would like something if it is a family heirloom.

The most important thing is to take action on those delayed decisions and aim to get your painting pile down in volume.

PHOTOGRAPHS

Decluttering and organising photographs is a mammoth task that we will never be able to do justice to in one small section of this chapter.

Photographs are arguably the most sentimental thing we have in life. When people are asked what they would take to a desert island, photographs win hands down every time.

They provide background, nuance and context to our lives and those surrounding us. If diaries are A-list, photographs are Oscar-winning when it comes to sentimental items, so radical decluttering is rarely on people's agendas.

But one thing is certain: not all photos are equal, and it's our job to sort, prioritise and categorise so they can be enjoyed now and in the future. People make photos come to life and although a panorama of the perfect sunset over Lake Garda is special, the ones that make you smile most will be the ones with you and your family or friends enjoying the sunset over Lake Garda.

The scope of a photograph project can be as small as gathering a heap of photos from the bottom of drawers and the back of cupboards and popping them into a sensible box, all the way up to scanning, digitising, adding metadata and creating back-ups.

If you choose to embark on a photo project here are a few basic but handy tips to help you on your way:

- As wrong as it may seem, it is possible to throw a photo away or hit that delete button!
- Decide on your categorisation early into the process – by person, by year, by theme?
- Investing in the right boxes and equipment to protect the most precious thing you own is worth every penny.
- Try to mirror your physical system in your digital one.
- Back up, back up and back up again for good measure.

And last but absolutely no means least, don't rush. Take your time and enjoy reconnecting with your photos. Doing a photo project brings great joy, and the knowledge you will easily be able to find what you want when you want it is a great comfort too.

Organisation and Storage

It's important to take a step back at this point and make a decision about how you'd like to enjoy your sentimental items in the future.

You will have thought about how to display or store things as you have been considering each category but now it's time to move to the next steps.

Sentimental items are there to be cherished, so if it is at all possible, let's facilitate bringing them into the everyday. Can special photos or letters go into a frame? Can we upcycle a piece of furniture so we can use it every day? Can we bind that special course we wrote so it has pride of place on a living room bookcase? Create that collage wall so you can have more memories at one time. These ideas are not easy to execute but they are possibilities that we can work towards one step at a time.

But, of course, there will also be things that don't belong out on display and need to be kept in a box. These are special items that deserve special boxes, so try and get hold of the best you can afford if you don't have them already. Lids are essential as these aren't things that will be accessed every day so need to be protected from the elements. And, as always, be sure the box is the optimum size for the things you need to store.

Considering how you are going to split your sentimental items is essential. If you have multiple family members it makes sense to have a box for each to allow you to pass them on with ease when it's time for them to move from your home elsewhere.

If you have space to store sentimental boxes in the body of your home that is the goal but if, like most people, your sentimental collection will be in a bulk-storage area or at the top of a cupboard, you may need a second temporary holding area. For example, if you have kids bringing home certificates or drawings with regularity but your sentimental collection is in your garage then you may need a holding area, such as an in-tray. Then, with regularity, you can go through the holding area to decide whether an item is sentimental enough to be kept long term in permanent storage.

If you are storing lots of paper-based items how are you going to categorise and sort them for easy retrieval? A chronological or thematic system works well and pop wallets provide a fantastic solution to keep things nicely together.

Grab your label maker and use terminology on your labels that will make sense to you and other people who may need access to your sentimental collection, either now or in the future. If you are storing sentimental items in an attic, basement or garage be sure to keep them off the floor and use larger labels on each side of the box.

And, finally, if you have memories that you don't want to share with anyone else, make that clear on your labels and keep your fingers crossed that people adhere to your wishes.

Now, we're going off-piste here and asking you to take a moment before 'the doing' is officially done. Why? Because this has been a chapter and a half. If you're still with us, well done for sticking with it.

In some ways, coming to terms with all the varied emotions relating to different categories of sentimental items is like doing your whole house all over again. Every category brings with it something new, so no wonder it can feel overwhelming.

Take some time to think about the different categories we have chatted through:

- Can you identify which category is going to be the most emotive for you?
- Do you have one category of items that you already know needs to be pared down significantly?
- Do you need to involve other family members in the process?
- Have you decided on the pacing of your project? Are you going to tackle it little and often or try and break the back of it quickly?

The Finishing Touches

We've executed a mammoth task now and you should be so proud. If an 'after' photo works, by all means take one. Run the vacuum round if needed and, of course, if you are donating any items, now's the time to make that happen.

But, most of all, the end of this task is all about reflection and sharing. You will have unearthed things you had forgotten about. Enjoy the opportunity to tell your stories to your loved ones or send that text with a funny photo you found. Savour every special memory and enjoy every poignant moment. Well done! You've made it!

13

Keeping the clutter at bay

'Little and often is the key.'

Oh my word – the end is in striking distance. The clutter is gone, the house is done, the decluttering muscle is strong and you're feeling good. We couldn't be happier for you. And who made this happen? You did. By following a process and learning to understand and challenge some of your lifelong behaviours. Tackling a whole house of clutter and changing your clutter mindset is no mean feat so we applaud your hard work and determination. Fantastic!

Before we move into maintenance mode, let's take a moment to think about whether you feel like your decluttering is complete or whether you would still like to dig a little deeper. At this stage you are armed with a greater degree of self-awareness when it comes to decluttering, and are hopefully delighted with your progress, but the task may not yet be fully complete. As you have made your way through the book and become more confident, you may now feel, on reflection, that you were able to declutter more thoroughly in the latter half of the book.

This is a very normal feeling to have and all part of the process. If you have struggled with clutter for much of your life, feeling a sense of control while decluttering is vital, and that's why we emphasise *if in doubt, don't throw it out*. But now perhaps you feel more in control of your decluttering journey. If this is you, then you may wish to revisit earlier chapters and rooms in this book to see if you can go further with your decluttering now that your decluttering muscle has strengthened.

You may reassess your kitchen and feel as if you would now be able to make different decisions about the things you kept, for example. There may be things you had decided not to throw out, and now you wonder why. You will always have a chance to refine and refresh. This is what we call a phased approach and we wholeheartedly recommend it. You may need a Phase 2, a Phase 3, even a Phase 10 in your home, but this is all part of the process. There are very few transformations where the results are perfect first time round. Take your time, revisit your previous rooms and see whether there are any other items that you now feel ready to make a different decision on. Fine-tuning is where the magic happens, and you will always be able to refer back to this book as a guide.

We'd like to take you back to our favourite mantra that we talked about way back on p. 16: If you always do what you've always done, you'll always get what you've always got.

You've certainly changed the way you've tackled your clutter during this process and the outcome should speak for itself. But now we'd love you to turn your attention to your ongoing, lifelong relationship to decluttering and organising. We want you to take all the incredible strategies you have learned on your journey and embed them in the everyday mechanics of running a household. The good news is you're starting with the most solid foundations possible with your freshly decluttered and organised home. Let's look now at how you can maintain your decluttered home; how you can keep the clutter at bay by establishing routines that will minimise the effort required to keep your home running like clockwork.

Things come into our homes on a weekly basis and, in order to retain the harmony we have created, things need to leave too. Stuff is largely transitory and we are the gatekeepers. We decide what comes in and what goes out. Our households change. Our homes change. Our tastes change and, most of all, our mindsets change. Once our mindsets change, decluttering becomes less about planning big sessions and more about stopping the clutter at source, about seeing and dealing with things as we notice them and about the ability to build short bursts of decluttering and organising into our every day. Let's look at ways you can support your ongoing decluttering moving forwards.

Creating your reset

To support your decluttering journey let us introduce you to a reset. A reset is a combination of tidying and cleaning that happens at least once, sometimes multiple times, a day. In a nutshell, a reset serves to return your newly decluttered and organised room or home back to the way you want it to be. In a bedroom, for example, a reset is likely to involve opening the curtains, making your bed and putting clothes away. In a kitchen it will be putting away the things you have used to make a meal, loading the dishwasher and wiping down work surfaces.

In order to effectively incorporate resets into your daily life, you need to consider the following:

Your household. How many things become out of place throughout the day in your household? Every home is different. The amounts vary hugely from just a few items to hundreds. Your number is going to be dictated by how many people are in your home, how old they are, how many things they like to use throughout the day and how focused they are on putting things away.

Your reality. Consider the amount of times you need to reset the house throughout the day. The nature of a household with small children, for example, means that the kids are likely to move through toys at a rate of knots throughout the day, so there is a greater need to do more regular resets. Are you careful to put things away after you use them or does your kitchen look like a bomb site once you've cooked a meal? Being realistic about the pressure put on to your home each day will allow you to determine the number of resets that make sense for you.

Your availability. It's important to be honest about your situation. When is the most appropriate time for you to do a reset – perhaps before work, on your lunch-break, after the school run or before bed? You might be thinking none of those times work well for you, but the reality is that at least one or two times of the day have to work. In order to keep your home orderly, resets are a must, so time has to be allocated to them. The last thing you want is for all your hard work decluttering and organising to go to waste, and for you to be back to square one within a few short weeks!

Non-negotiables

Your reset will comprise what we call non-negotiables. A non-negotiable is exactly what it says on the tin: it absolutely must be done as part of a reset – no ifs, no buts. And although there are some non-negotiables that are common to every home, you need to spend some time thinking about what yours are and how often you need to incorporate them into your reset routine. Let's give some examples:

Putting on a load of laundry. How often would you need to wash clothes to keep things ticking through rather than having to do mountains at once? And don't forget the drying and putting away phases either.

Putting on the dishwasher or doing the washing up. How many dishes do you go through in a day? Do you need to put on more than one dishwasher load? Are you able to fill your dishwasher during the day? Are you happy to do your dishes after your evening meal is done, but leave a few random glasses and cups from the late evening until the following day? It's important to establish your own standards and attempt to adhere to them.

When are you going to make your bed? Before you shower, after you shower, after it's aired, after the school run? All of these seemingly little details are vital to ensure your non-negotiables are specific, achievable and timely.

How often do you need to sweep, vacuum or mop the kitchen to keep it looking presentable? Different people have different levels of tolerance when it comes to cleanliness and tidiness, so the key is finding your sweet spot.

At what time of day are you going to reset your children's toys? If they have a dedicated play space, perhaps once a day is enough. If they are using toys in communal spaces, this may need to happen more frequently.

There are so many tasks that could appear on your non-negotiable list. And there will be a different non-negotiable list for each of the high-traffic rooms in your home.

Remember the list you come up with should not be governed by your desire to do a task. A regular reset is dictated by identifying your own personal standards and avoids tasks becoming mammoth and overwhelming. Little and often is the key. And so is learning and practising delegation.

Using a Timer

Before you can determine when is a good time to incorporate daily resets into your schedule, you first need to understand how long something is likely to take. We have a habit of over- or underestimating the duration of a chore.

How long does it take to make the bed and open the curtains? How long does it take to get the recycling into the garage? Our kitchen reset may have felt never-ending in the past, but that was before you cleared the decks and learned to live with less, so the chances are it will take much less time than previously. But you need to have a clear picture of how long rather than a guesstimate. Knowledge is power. By timing each of your non-negotiables and assigning them to a time of day, when you can find the time to do them, you are setting yourself up for greater success.

Timers can also be useful as a motivational tool. You can use a timer to hold yourself accountable and keep you motivated. Finding a short slot each day to spend on resetting your home will save you hours at the weekend. And now that you have the solid foundations in place for a clutter-free home, you could also use timers to target specific areas for revisiting your decluttering every now and then too.

Habit Forming

Throughout this book, we have repeatedly reinforced the idea that by doing the thinking first we are armed with a greater understanding of the task in hand, and we will then become better equipped to do the doing. And resets are no exception.

As we establish our daily resets, we need to spend time analysing what has worked and what hasn't previously to allow us to progress and move forwards.

By repeatedly doing daily resets, they will gradually become cemented as part of our daily routines too. Like any habit, it takes a while for them to form and take hold, but once you have established the parameters of your reset and start to practise, day after day, they no longer feel like a chore. Making your bed fits into place as easily as brushing your teeth.

Keeping up momentum

One of the biggest issues when it comes to creating and maintaining a home you want to be in is retaining your focus on decluttering and organising when life gets in the way. Long term, it just needs to slot in alongside all the other elements of normal life, so now it's time to work out how to keep your momentum going as and when needed.

There's honestly no secret formula, no life hack, no rocket science. The way to keep momentum going is to remember the key components of the decluttering and organising process that we have outlined in this book. Let's just remind you of all the factors that are going to help you live the clutter-free life you've been yearning for:

Have a vision of the person you will be when you are free of clutter. How do you want to spend your time when you are not a slave to stuff and chores? Keep your big-picture goal front of mind at all times and especially when this journey starts to feel insurmountable.

Realism is everything in a decluttering journey. Be realistic about your life, your world, your home, your constraints, your energy levels and your clutter personality and it will set you up for greater success.

Consistency is way more impactful than intensity. We talked about having undergone a burst of activity during this decluttering process but let's always be mindful to keep those bursts manageable and sensible. That way, you can do another burst tomorrow, and the next day, and the day after that.

Recognise when you are allowing perfectionism to hold you back. Done is always better than perfect. Perfectionism and procrastination go hand in hand and sometimes we just need to give things a go and not overthink.

Your decluttering journey will ebb and flow. There will be days when you feel you are winning the race. There will be other days when you feel you didn't even make it off the starting blocks. Every day provides a fresh opportunity for a personal best. Celebrate every emotion you recognise, celebrate every item you let go of, celebrate every reset you undertake.

Document your journey. Take photos, write down your feelings, struggles and actions to remind yourself of your goals, wins and woes. Having a clear picture of where you want to get to and how far you've come is a powerful tool to keep you on track.

Connect with like-minded people. Having people around you who understand the challenges faced by people who struggle with clutter is validating. The Declutter Hub community is supportive, non-judgemental, kind and knowledgeable, so if you haven't found them yet, now's the time. You can find all the details you need on p. 250.

Continue to fine-tune. Even the most orderly of homes needs a refresh from time to time. If things go awry and you feel your clutter is getting out of control again, don't panic. Think first about what it was about the Reset Your Home system that was the key to unlocking your progress. Re-read the thinking sections if you see clutter creeping back in. Re-read the doing sections if your organisational systems are threatening to break down. And if you're not sure, read the chapter relating to the room you're struggling with or check the index to help guide you. This book can serve as your point of reference when life gets in the way.

14

Final thoughts

So, we are nearing the end of our deep dive into our emotions-based decluttering journey with you. We've been working in this crazy world of decluttering for years now and love every single moment. We never tire of seeing journeys unfold and progress happen. We feel privileged to help people fall back in love with their homes each and every day.

There are two stages of each decluttering journey that never fail to blow us away.

The first is when you have the momentous realisation that what has been holding you back is in fact not an overabundance of stuff but your deep-seated emotional connection to stuff. It's a game-changer. Always remember, emotions first, stuff second.

The second is when the penny finally drops that decluttering is not about having less stuff. It's about the effect that living with less has on your day-to-day life. Less stuff equals more calm. Less stuff equals more space. Less stuff equals more money. Less stuff equals more time. And rather than something to fear, less stuff is something to be celebrated.

While it may sound strange, we have always considered putting stuff in a bin bag and carting it off for donation to be a by-product of the decluttering process. The real success lies in the desire and ability to keep the clutter at bay, to enjoy what you have at home and to seek out only those things that serve you in the here and now. That change in mindset is the ultimate goal, and you have the tools to do this now.

When you unravel your personal relationship to stuff and are excited to live with less, you've just found the golden ticket to a life-changing transformation.

Thank you for trusting in us to guide you on your journey. You've got this!

Appendix

A note on paperwork

Paperwork is a huge contributor to household clutter and will undoubtedly be something you come across while you are working in your home. As we have mentioned, paperwork is complex, unwieldy and time-consuming and for this reason isn't included in this book. That said, we'd love to give you some very basic advice that will help you later down the line.

As you come across paperwork, leave it to one side until after you have organised the rest of your home unless it's something that needs to be dealt with immediately.

There are no definitive answers about how long to keep paperwork for. The real answer lies with you. How long would you like to keep different categories of paperwork?

Do, however, try to move out of your comfort zone step by step and try to live with less.

Evaluate where your paperwork is currently, what is working and what is not. If your current filing system no longer works, it's time for you think about changing it.

Embrace technology, paperless options and apps. Once you spend time working with them, they make life much simpler.

Have clearly defined roles and responsibilities in your household about who deals with what.

Use labels for organisation and information.

Acknowledgements

From Ingrid

To my amazing mum, Loni, who taught me everything I know about decluttering, organising, cleaning and keeping things tidy.

To my wonderful husband, Jan, whose unwavering support, knowledge and love inspire me every day to keep going.

To my fabulous kids, Max and Anne, who listen to me each and every day chat about the decluttering world and are always there to help me in any way they can.

To my family and friends, thank you for your encouragement and belief in me, way before being a Professional Organiser was 'a thing'.

To my Organise Your House team – for being such wonderful ambassadors.

To Mylene – the best accountability partner and buddy I could ever have asked for.

From Lesley

To Luke, Leah, Nathan and Ellie – for being my biggest cheerleaders, putting up with my endless Declutter Hub chat and surviving life so far with a very distracted mum.

To my dad, Dave – thank you for keeping me on my toes and always being so proud of 'Our Les'.

To my father-in-law, John – for caring so much about the book, the business and me.

To Christine, Julie and Jenny – thanks for the fun, the wine and the endless chats on the Bridgewater Canal.

To Katie and my dedicated and fabulous Clutter Fairy team – you inspire me every day.

And finally to Steve – the kindest, most inspirational and honest man I am lucky to call my husband. Please promise me you'll read this book and make me an even happier wife.

From us both

To Holly and Sarah – we feel so incredibly lucky to have such calm, supportive and encouraging editors. Our meetings were always such a highlight. You and the entire Bloomsbury team have made this process enriching and exciting. Thank you for seeing the possibility in our podcast ramblings and making sure our words are the very best they can be.

To Ros – for keeping the wheels of the Declutter Hub turning every day and allowing us to do our thing while you do all the hard work. We appreciate you!

To Luke a.k.a Peek – another shout out to you for the incredible illustrations that have brought our words to life. It's the icing on our very special cake.

And last but certainly not least, to you, our readers. We feel sure you'll find a little piece of yourself in each chapter as you read it, and we hope that thought by thought, room by room and day by day the clutter will disappear and the calm will appear.

An invitation

After making so much progress in your home and your clutter mindset, you may be feeling you want more! And luckily, we can help you with that. If you're not in our Declutter Hub world already, we'd love you to join us.

Join our Declutter Hub membership
If you want to go deeper, tackle some of the areas we haven't covered, or want to tap into a community full of like-minded people all united in their struggle and progress with clutter, we'd love to invite you to join our Declutter Hub membership.

Here you'll receive in-depth help and expertise, support, inspiration, friendship and laughter. Everyone is at different stages of their decluttering journey and is eager to share their experience to help others make the same progress.

We have an abundance of tools available that will give you everything you need in your quest for a clutter free home. Check out members.declutterhub.com for more information and we hope to see you on the inside.

Listen to our free weekly podcast
If it's related to decluttering and organising, we've probably talked about it! We have hundreds of weekly episodes all ready and waiting for you. Our aim is to educate and inspire you and also to add the fun factor into decluttering. You'll find it at declutterhub.com/podcast or by searching for the Declutter Hub podcast wherever you listen to your podcasts.

Connect with us on socials
We have a thriving Facebook group, a Facebook page, Instagram and YouTube. A search for the Declutter Hub will find us, we're sure.

Grab some free stuff
We have some great checklists to help you feel in control of your decluttering, so hover over the QR code below and it will take you to the checklists and all our other resources in one handy place.

Index